NOT
ANOTHER
RICH
IDEA

Turning Riches Into Wealth

NOT
ANOTHER
RICH
IDEA

Turning Riches Into Wealth

EUGENE STRITE

Generation Culture Transformation
Specializing in publishing for generation culture change

eGenCo. LLC
824 Tallow Hill Road
Chambersburg, PA- 17202, USA
Phone: 717-461-3436
email: info@egenco.com
Website: www.egenco.com
        www.egenbooks.com

facebook.com/egenbooks
twitter.com/vishaljets
youtube.com/egenpub
egenco.com/blog

Paperback ISBN 978-1-936554-08-9
eBook ISBN 978-1-936554-09-6

First Printing: 2011

Cover Design by Ambert Rodriguez, www.guezworks.com
Text Design and Typesetting by Kevin Lepp, www.kmlstudio.com

This book is dedicated to my beautiful wife, Karen, who is my best friend and partner in all our endeavors. She is my strongest supporter and has provided great insight in the refinement of this book. I am thankful for her constant encouragement and the balance that I need in all aspects of my life. I also dedicate this book to my late father-in-law, Arthur F. Lehman, who taught and trained me in the ways of finance, trade, and industry, revealing to me the danger of transacting business according to conventional standards. I am grateful for these strong foundations upon which my businesses are based today. Finally, this book is dedicated to each of my children—Selena, Wesley, Sherah, and Sheila—who constantly challenge me to view the world differently. I am so proud of each of them.

ACKNOWLEDGMENTS

My heartfelt gratitude and appreciation goes out to my wife, Karen—you are the love of my life. Thank you for 37 wonderful years of marriage and for your encouragement and support. Selena, Wesley, Sherah and Sheila—you are the four best children a father could ask for; each of you have a huge contribution to make to the world. To Mom and Dad, I am grateful for your commitment to raising your children with values, and for your genuine concern for the interests of others. To my son-in-law, Vishal Jetnarayan, thank you for encouraging me to write yet another book. Without your administrative skills, this endeavor probably wouldn't have happened. And finally, to my friends around the world—thank you all for the deposits you have made to my life.

INTRODUCTION

Your success in life is not about what you possess, and it is not found in titles or degrees. Your success has everything to do with what you pass on to future generations. Many have accomplished much—appearing successful—only to die and be forgotten because they did not have in mind the coming generation. True success is not only what you accumulate for yourself, but what you pass on to those who will come after you.

In Not Another Rich Idea, I desire to lay out a plan and purpose for wealth creation. It is a misconception to think that the wealthy are born lucky or with a silver spoon in their mouths. On the contrary, personal wealth development requires discipline. Discipline is the pathway to maturity, and maturity is required to resist the whims and pleasurable thoughts that prevent many people from increasing their wealth over time.

Wealth is neither the enemy nor the master of humanity. While those in society seem to rule the masses because of their great wealth, the source of that wealth—a creative mind—is the true key. We all have creative minds, but many are not willing (or are not disciplined) to develop their minds or use their creativity. They would rather allow others to think for them. So, while the masses are controlled by a few, and those few typically have great wealth, it is their discipline to cultivate a creative mind that has placed them in positions of influence.

The greatest gift that money awards us is the ability to fulfill the dreams that are in our hearts. Those who feel that they are entitled to what they did not work for will always be poor, never experiencing the joy of living or the free expression of those creative juices that are bottled up inside. Instead, entitlement causes us to use all of our energy to pursue and possess money and things. Ironically, in our pursuit to possess and control those things—money or otherwise—we end up being possessed and controlled by them!

We must come face to face with our understanding of money, its purpose, and how it relates to our destinies. We must realize that we, each, individually, are the CEOs of our own lives, and that where we are today is a direct result of the decisions we have made—good and bad—along the way. What we think and say about money has resulted in our experience with it.

Wealth is simply the natural increase of what we have invested in. It doesn't just happen. Discipline and careful planning make the difference between wealth and poverty. This poverty is first a reality in our minds, which controls our speech and our thoughts.

Change your thoughts and your speech about money, and your bottom line will also change. Change nothing, and nothing will change, including your bottom line. The money will grow according to your discipline to save and invest. As it grows, follow your heart, sow into the next generation, and your life will be one of significance.

In the next two years, if you are willing to do what others are not willing to do—discipline yourself to save and invest—you will be able to do for the rest of your life what others cannot for the rest of theirs.

Eugene Strite

TABLE OF CONTENTS

YOU GOTTA SERVE SOMEBODY

CHAPTER ONE

Today, in this age of nanotechnology and milliseconds, our human brains are still only able to hold one thought at a time. We aren't programmed with multitasking chips like some kind of computer; and no matter how hard we try, we cannot think two thoughts at the same time. Yes, we may be able to switch back and forth between thoughts rapidly, but we are not able to hold two thoughts simultaneously no matter how smart or well educated we are. Try it. Can you totally focus your mind on a dog and a horse at the same time? Can you think about what you're going to eat for dinner, while considering what is ahead of you at work tomorrow? We are just not designed to hold two thoughts at exactly the same time.

The same is true about what we serve. In the simplest sense, to serve something or somebody is to make that thing or person the focus of our lives. Contrary to what many people believe, to say that we cannot serve two masters means that we cannot truly give primary allegiance to more than one object or priority in our lives. We might have many interests and many priorities that we try to balance from day to day, but one will invariably take precedence over the others. So let me ask you: who or what are you serving?

Who or what is master of your life? Are you serving a higher power? Are you serving some religious cause or organization? Are you serving your family? Are you serving the state? Or are you serving yourself? Any or all of these (as well as others) may be relevant in your life, but one will be dominant over the others. Who or what takes top priority in your life?

Everybody Serves Somebody

What we serve motivates our lives, dictating what we think and how we respond in various situations. We cannot truly be motivated by two things at the same time; one or the other is in control. No one can serve two masters. We usually think of a "master" as a person, but the word applies also to anything that controls us. I can be mastered or motivated by love or by greed, but not by both at the same time. I will compromise one or the other.

In a personal and human sense, our "master" is the one who is in charge of our lives. It is the master who decides what we will eat and when we will sleep. It is the master who will determine whom we marry and how we live. It is the master who decides how and where we spend our money. The master is the one who owns us. In reality, we do not have a master; the master has us.

To serve implies the existence of a master to be served. In this sense, the word serve closely resembles the meaning of the word worship. That which we serve with our highest devotion, whether person or thing, becomes like a god to us. Whatever we serve controls and maintains power over our lives because we allow that control and power due to the value we place on the object of our service (worship). Many times we struggle financially because of what we have decided to serve. In the financial realm, as in every other arena of life, everybody serves somebody.

Bob Dylan, a famous American folk singer and songwriter, expressed this truth in one of his songs:

You may be an ambassador to England or France,
You may like to gamble, you might like to dance,
You may be the heavyweight champion of the world,
You may be a socialite with a long string of pearls.

But you're gonna have to serve somebody, yes indeed.
You're gonna have to serve somebody.
Well, it may be the devil or it may be the Lord,
But you're gonna have to serve somebody.

And there are clear-cut ways to determine who or what we serve.

Knowing What We Serve
You Serve What You Value

If we want to find out who or what someone serves, we need only to look at what he or she values. We know what we value by what we carry in our pockets and in our hearts.

Unfortunately, we often place value on those things that are not in the least bit valuable. Many of the items we value are perishable. They will not survive beyond this lifetime, and often pass away much sooner than that. And yet, millions of people consume their lives and substance by incessantly pursuing objects that will neither last nor bring lasting happiness or contentment. Wise men through the ages have taught that the greatest happiness in life comes from pursuing meaningful ideas, causes, and values of lasting worth, which transcend our own selfish desires and pursuits. So why should we want to devote the short and precious years of our lives striving for materials

> **You know what you serve by what you value—by whatever claims your money, time, attention, and passion.**

3

that will disappear in time?

We have filled our lives and our storage places with possessions we believe to be valuable and important. Yet in time, they are constantly being replaced with new layers of "invaluable treasures." It's peculiar that what we value changes so often. Just look at pictures of yourself or your parents two decades ago. Look at the hairstyles and clothing of the day. The fact that what seems to be valuable to the world changes so often is an indication that those items have little or no true value at all. Only that which lasts beyond our own lifetime is really valuable.

> *Only that which lasts beyond our own lifetime is really valuable.*

You Serve That Which Claims Your Time and Money

There is probably no greater indication of what we are serving than by where and how we invest our time and money. What we serve determines our priorities. If impressing other folks is important to us, then we will spend money to do so. If building a legacy that will benefit and prosper our children, their children, and many generations to come is important, then we will devote our time, energy, and resources to that end. No matter how busy we are or how much money we have, we will make time and set aside resources for what we value the most.

Many people spend their time and lives working to pile up more stuff to fill their closets and storage places, while they relinquish the care of their children to others. There is nothing wrong with both parents having to work to provide for necessities, such as food and clothing, but many times they work to purchase another vacation or an extra vehicle for pleasure. They are in effect serving the car they drive, or the vacation, or whatever "goods" they are working for.

4

If children are important to us, we will spend time with them. I don't recall hearing of any deathbed confessions where a person expresses regret for not having spent enough time at the office or not winning an athletic competition, or not having a nicer house; but we may regret not having spent enough time with our children and families.

One of the not-so-funny ironies is that we end up serving the objects that are meant to serve us. We become addicted to "stuff" at the expense of our relationships at every level. In our crazed obsession with keeping up appearances and always having the newest and latest gadget or appliance or technology, we threaten our own retirement stability, not to mention our children's future prosperity, by failing to save and to plan ahead. Our misguided devotion to worthless articles prevents us from focusing on what truly matters the most.

The unfortunate fact is that even in the most materially prosperous nations on earth, many people devote the majority of their labor and income to servicing debt instead of planning for the future. We must realize that this is oppression. To whatever degree your future income is committed to current expenses is the degree of your financial bondage. Whatever you serve you will have to feed like a pony living in your backyard. What kinds of "ponies" are tied up in your backyard?

You Serve What Commands Your Attention

One way to realize what has hold of your focus is to ask yourself what you look forward to most when you get out of bed in the morning. Do you look forward to reading about your local sports, or to developing your mind and character through such activities as religious devotions and exercises, or reading literature that stimulates your mind and inner being? In other words, do you look forward to feeding your belly or your spirit? Do you live only for the moment, or do you live for the future? What stimulates you? What are you passionate about? What things do you always make room for in your schedule and in your budget?

The most successful people—as well as the happiest and most fulfilled—are those who have established a priority in their lives that drives, informs, and influences everything they do. The same should be true for us. We sometimes reason that we are too busy to focus. Often our lives are overloaded with social, religious, and community obligations, in addition to work responsibilities and family needs. But are we busier than anyone else? Many of the most successful and fulfilled people in the world are also some of the busiest. The secret to their success is that they have learned to establish priorities in their lives so that they can focus on what is most important and not get distracted by less important objects. In the same way, the secret to our success is a matter of choosing our priorities. We will give our attention to whatever seems to be the most urgent to our survival. Maybe that is why many of us are doing little more than surviving, not to mention prospering. We have focused our time, money, attention, and energy on the wrong things.

> *The most successful people as well as the happiest and most fulfilled are those who have established a priority in their lives that drives, informs, and influences everything they do.*

One of the consequences of giving our attention to items that really don't matter is that we begin to worry. Consequently, worry can tie up our minds so that we cannot do anything productive. When we worry, we hold a negative view of the future, which makes us frantic and doubtful as to whether we will find what we need for tomorrow. The antidote to worry comes in understanding who we are, why we are here, what is most important, and then living our lives accordingly.

Here's the bottom line: worry is not a very generous emotion to serve. Worry drags us down a hole and keeps us visionless and powerless. When we are focused only on what we do not have or what we might not understand about the future, we will inevitably miss the richness of the life in front of us today. When we live under worry, we will not be able to see either opportunities or obstacles.

Making the Choice

You have a choice to make, and it is one of the most important choices you will ever make. It is not only important for you, but also for the generations to come. The choice you make will determine what kind of legacy you will leave behind for your children.

You will know what you serve by what you value—by whatever claims your money, time, attention, and passion. The way you handle your finances provides evidence as to whom or what you are serving. This is a point I will reinforce again and again in this book. Money itself is not evil. There is nothing wrong with acquiring and enjoying material possessions—as long as you do not allow your desire for them to control you.

Money is not the problem. The difficulty comes with how tight a grip money has on your heart. Ancient wisdom tells us that it is not money itself, but the love of money that is the root of evil.

So, you have a choice to make. Are you going to serve money and material gain, or will you devote yourself to serving a higher good? You cannot take money or material goods with you when you die, but you can use them to help build a lasting legacy for your children and future generations. In order to do so, you must learn to establish proper priorities and come to a clear understanding of money and how it works. That is the aim of this book.

1. Bob Dylan, Gotta Serve Somebody (Special Rider Music; 1979), http://www.bobdylan.com/#/songs/gotta-serve-somebody.

SHARING WITH OTHERS

CHAPTER TWO

The collapse of the Soviet Union in the early 1990s brought upheaval into the lives of millions of Europeans. Euphoria over newfound freedom quickly mingled with fear of the breakdown of social order. Hope for the future was tempered by uncertainty over the present. Triumph or tragedy, everyone had a story. One young man, an artist, struggled for nearly two years to survive as a beggar on the streets of an eastern European city. One day, moved at the sight of two other beggars in similar circumstances to his own, he counted out the biggest coins he had and divided them between the two. Soon after this, someone bought not one, but two, of the lovely little paintings he was selling. This was the beginning of his rise out of poverty. What made the difference? Reflecting on what had happened, the young artist remembered reading ancient words of wisdom that said that those who give generously will receive in turn. It was then that he realized the true value and power of giving.

In fact, giving is the most important principle for achieving true and lasting success. Does that surprise you? Do you find it hard to accept the idea that a key to establishing financial success in your own life is that you learn to give away your financial resources? This may seem to defy human logic, but it has been proven over and over in history, based on the ancient principle that it is better to give than to receive.

> *Giving is the most important principle for achieving true and lasting success.*

The road to financial success begins with adjusting your mind-set to think in terms of generosity toward others rather than selfishly hoarding your resources. As counterintuitive as it may seem to a "rational" human mind, giving is a fundamental principle of financial success.

Give, Give, Give

Another word for money is currency. Related to the word current, currency carries the idea of movement, as with water in a river—something that flows. And just like water, money that does not move becomes stale and stagnant. It needs to move frequently in order to remain fresh and productive.

For this reason, we should be channels through which the finances of the world flow, not people who hoard money. Hoarding money and being selfish stops the flow. It creates clogged pipes, so to speak. Generosity begets generosity. The way to get the flow going again in your life is to start giving. Open the valve; be generous! Give extra tips. Make a deliberate choice to invest in others and then watch what happens!

An ancient proverb says that a man who gives freely will prosper, and that a man who refreshes others will himself be refreshed. In this sense, give literally means "to scatter abroad," in the sense of a farmer sowing seed, as in the ancient manner. To "scatter" means "to distribute irregularly—to strew or cast in all directions." Farmers in ancient times walked their fields with a bag of seed, casting handfuls of seed far and wide in every direction. Liberality was the rule; the more seed sown, the larger the harvest. Farmers who were stingy with their seed could expect only a meager return.

In the same way, scattering implies that you need to open your hands and release your seed liberally, and have confidence that the generosity you show not only will help others but will return to you in greater measure.

This whole idea seems backward or even crazy to our logical reasoning. How is it possible to get more by throwing away what we have? It makes no sense to our rational mind, which

> *You need to open your hands and release your seed liberally, and have confidence that the generosity you show will not only help others but will return to you in greater measure.*

wants to hold onto everything we have with a tight grip. But you were born to let go, just as a baby bird perched on the edge of its mother's nest prepares to let go and fly. It was born to soar, but it will never experience that exhilaration until it lets go and fills its wings with air. There is something beyond the perceived safety of the nest. You also were born to soar, but you must let go of what you hold onto so stubbornly. There is something more to be gained than what you are afraid to let go of. There is more to life than simply feathering your own nest.

Giving does more for the giver than for the receiver. It truly is more blessed to give than to receive. Giving and receiving are in fact two sides of the same coin. Giving is an issue of the heart.

> *There is great joy in giving freely because when you give to others, you grow within yourself.*

There is great joy in giving freely because when you give to others, you grow within yourself. Selfishness leads to an inward focus on yourself, which eventually causes your spirit to shrivel away.

Although personal benefit

11

should never be your primary motivation for giving, it is true nevertheless that generosity in giving brings back abundant returns to the giver.

One of the best uses to which we can put our money and other financial resources is to share with those who are less fortunate than we are. Giving can be a very enriching and rewarding experience. Everyone, regardless of income, should learn to be a giver. Giving is the best way to keep material possessions in the right perspective in our lives. We need to give as a guard against greed and selfishness. Sharing with others helps keep our heart in the right place.

Why do we put so much value in money—metal discs or pieces of paper bearing the faces of dead rulers? We are held in bondage to them and thereby lack power and provision. In most cases, it is not that we have money, but that money has us. There is nothing more liberating to the soul than to be free of the love of money and to walk with power and purpose in life, no longer possessed by dead men's faces. One so liberated naturally enters into a life characterized by liberality.

True wealth does not come from what you hold onto, but from what you give away. Wealth is more than wages; it is abundance, and abundance is meant to be shared. Generous giving demonstrates that you are free from fear, and freedom from fear is a blessing in itself.

> **True wealth does not come from what you hold onto, but from what you give away.**

How Should You Give?

Your giving, first of all, should be balanced. The resources available to you include more than just money. You must find the proper balance between giving your money, your time, and your assets. There are times certainly when you should give money, but sometimes the best gift you can give to another person is the gift of your time.

In addition to balance, your giving should be sensitive to the needs and situations of others. There are some people and situations that each of us is perfectly suited to help. Needs that you can meet and encouragement you can give are all around you. All you have to do is open your eyes.

> *You must find the proper balance between giving your money, your time, and your assets.*

Before giving large sums of money, committing sizable chunks of time, or parting with major assets, it is vitally important that spouses, or partners in any type of relationship, be in agreement with one another. Financial matters cause more problems and conflict than any other single issue. For this reason, couples or business partners should take time to discuss matters together very carefully before making a sizable gift.

Many people maintain a core belief that the more they give away, the less they will have. This erroneous assumption is called the "fixed pie" theory. "There is only so much to go around, and I must hold onto mine. Otherwise, I'll run out, and then where will I be?" Sometimes this attitude masquerades under the guise of being a "good manager." However, good managers are careful, thrifty, and responsible with their resources…but they are not stingy. Some people do not give to others because they do not think those others are worthy, or because they disapprove of their lifestyle, or because they feel those others already have enough or have misused what they were given. All of these "reasons" reflect a judgmental and prejudicial spirit. Still, we should give unselfishly to others—to honor and contribute to others, even as we ourselves have flourished and enjoyed a measure of success. We must be careful when evaluating others' "worthiness" to receive our generosity. Striking the proper balance between generosity and responsibility calls for wisdom, discretion, and careful discernment.

We should give with four basic dispositions in mind: willingly, regularly or systematically, cheerfully, and generously.

Willingly – this means giving of your own free will, without coercion, and not from a sense of guilt or obligation. Another way to approach this is to never look at what you have in order to determine what you are to give, but determine what you are to give and then take it from what you have. It is foolish to trust or put your hope in wealth. Material wealth is a tool, a means to an end. It is not and must never become an end in itself.

Regularly or Systematically – Systematic giving means to give in an orderly manner, constant, methodical, without varying; in other words, purposefully regular. Your giving should be planned and deliberate, treated with the same care and attention you give to paying your monthly bills. Don't approach your giving in a haphazard manner. Plan ahead. You will never give regularly and systematically unless you deliberately set up a plan to do so.

Cheerfully – Giving that makes a difference is more about attitude than amount. Whatever we give, and however much or little we give, we should give cheerfully. A cheerful spirit is a healthy spirit, and to give generously from a cheerful heart builds our character and enlarges our capacity to love, to be loved, and to enjoy the fullness of life.

Generously – The more generously you give, the more generous will be the returns. This is a simple but fundamental principle that exemplifies the law of sowing and reaping. A farmer who sows only a little seed can expect only a small harvest. A bountiful harvest in the future requires the generous sowing of much seed in the present. This principle is just as true in giving as it is in farming. If you want to be blessed with abundance tomorrow, give generously today.

To Whom Should You Give?

This is a valid question because of the enormous number of people, groups, and institutions that are always clamoring for our support. Some of them are worthy; many of them are not. We must exercise careful discernment in deciding where to invest our gifts.

Local charitable organizations and groups. It is important that you give to local organizations whose goal is to help others in your own community. I believe that if you give, not only will others benefit because of your giving, but you, too, will be rewarded.

National and worldwide agencies. You also should maintain a global outlook and be conscious to the needs of people around the world, while making sure that the money you give is actually being spent on the needs rather than being used to cover excessive administrative costs or support extravagant lifestyles of leaders of organizations. Do some research before you give. Agencies with nothing to hide will hide nothing. They will be transparent in accounting for their use of the gifts they receive.

Those in need. Needy people are all around us, including widows, orphans, poverty-stricken, physically and mentally disabled, and those suffering from all types of abuse. All you have to do is look. The needs are far too numerous for any of us to meet them all, so you must use wisdom and good judgment to decide who is most appropriate for you to help.

What Happens When We Do Not Give?

Wise people of every nationality and throughout every age of history have testified that the greatest satisfaction and fulfillment in life results from living generously toward others. When we do not give, we shut ourselves off from being of any use to anybody else.

When we make little or no effort to help others, we subsequently become even more calloused to their needs. Living only for riches and material possessions is an empty, lonely, unsatisfying existence. Those for whom money is the primary driving force of life are never satisfied, no matter how much money they have. Money is their master, and they are enslaved to their insatiable appetite for more. Those who master their money, on the other hand, are never enslaved by it; and their willingness to share generously of their substance produces peace and contentment in their hearts.

Be a Giver

Giving from a generous heart is the key to a successful, fruitful, and satisfying life. So be a giver! You will bring happiness to others, and consequently, you will prosper even more.

Winston Churchill, the great twentieth century British statesman, said, "We make a living by what we get; we make a life by what we give." Are you making a living, or are you making a life? Become a giver! It will change your life as well as the lives of those who benefit from your generosity.

> *We make a living by what we get; we make a life by what we give.*
>
> *Winston Churchill*

You Reap
What You Sow

Chapter Three

Several years ago, my wife and I invested in a small farm in south-central Pennsylvania. We purchased the farm not merely for our own enjoyment, but also with the expectation of it yielding some kind of return and producing a harvest. After we acquired the property, I walked among the fields to determine what we should sow that would provide the greatest return. That spring we planted barley.

We were blessed with a great harvest in the fall. As we harvested the barley, I picked up a single stalk and carefully counted 90 seeds—nearly a hundred-fold increase. Each one of those seeds, if sown back into the field, would yield at least 90 more seeds. In addition, the straw that remained after the barley was separated from the stalk was sold to provide even more profit. All in all, it was a very good year.

Our experience with our small farm illustrates a principle that every farmer knows, but which applies equally in every walk of life: You cannot expect an increase unless you first sow the seed. This is wisdom that has been acknowledged since ancient times. You reap what you sow.

The principle of sowing and reaping is familiar to most of

us, even to those who are not involved in gardening or farming. Common sense tells us that unless we plant seeds we will not reap a harvest. This is true in virtually every arena of human endeavor, not just agriculture. If we want to grow, we have to sow. We perform an act of kindness in the hope of getting kindness in return. Then, there is the act of planting a seed in the ground with the expectation of someday cutting a flower or eating a tomato. And the more liberally we sow, or the more widely we scatter our seed, the greater our potential for an abundant harvest.

Sowing and reaping is just as important a principle in finances as it is in any other area of life. The size and quality of your future harvest of financial prosperity depends on the quality and liberality of the financial seeds you sow today, not just in terms of planning, saving, and investing, but also in giving. Remember, generosity begets generosity.

> *The size and quality of your future harvest of financial prosperity depends on the quality and liberality of the financial seeds you sow today in terms of planning, saving, investing, and giving.*

In order better to understand the principle of sowing and reaping, we need to take a closer look at each separate element: 1. The Seed, 2. Sowing, and 3. Reaping.

The Seed

The seed is the source of life. It is the basis, the foundation, the fundamental unit of reproduction and increase.

Every living thing comes from a seed: trees, plants of all kind, man, animals, insects. Each has a seed of some kind or another. If there were no seed, the species would become extinct. That seed holds the pattern, the DNA for all the life that will descend from it. However, that DNA cannot be released until the seed is planted and dies.

Life is released in death. When a seed is planted in the earth and "dies," it is in reality transformed into something much greater—new life that produces much fruit.

As you make a living and endeavor to build a solid financial future for yourself and your family, remember that there will be no growth and no harvest without first having a seed to sow in the form of giving or investing.

Seed type and seed quality determine the nature of the crop. Good seed produces a good crop in kind; bad seed produces a bad crop (if it produces at all).

> *The purpose of financial seed is to produce a harvest of life, prosperity, and good works, not just for ourselves and our families, but for others as well.*

The nature of the crop we desire will determine the kind and quality of seed we sow. The purpose of financial seed is to produce a harvest of life, prosperity, and good works, not just for ourselves and our families, but for others as well.

In every apple, there is a seed. In the seed is the tree. In the tree are many more apples with even more seeds, which produce orchards of trees. It is the same with the fruit of our lives, our time, our hearts, our abilities, and our finances. In each area a seed is brought forth, which we must sow in some form or fashion.

> *Every resource we possess is a seed: time, money, kindness, love, gifts, talents. All of these, when sown into fertile ground, will produce an increase.*

Every resource we possess is a seed: time, money, kindness, love, gifts, talents. All of these, when sown into fertile ground, will produce an increase.

Through my own experiences over the years in observing

and counseling many people about their finances, I have become convinced that those who remain challenged and poor often do so because they consume their entire seed, leaving them with nothing left to sow.

Sowing

When I sow a seed, it yields fruit containing the same kind of seed. For example, if I sow a seed of kindness, it may not bring an immediate harvest; but if I am patient, I will eventually see an increase. The harvest we reap depends on the seed we sow. A seed of kindness begets kindness. Love begets love. Generosity begets generosity. On the other hand, hatred begets hatred, violence begets violence, and strife and division beget strife and division. Our world is already full enough of strife, violence, and hatred. If we want to see greater harvests of love, kindness, and generosity in our world, and especially in our own neighborhoods, we must sow the appropriate seeds in abundance. It is amazing how even some of the hardest and most frightening-looking people can melt when treated consistently with sincere love and kindness.

> *The harvest we reap depends on the seed we sow.*

The seed represents the future. What you have today is your future in seed form, and what you do with what you have today will determine your tomorrow. But in order for your seed to produce, it must be planted or sown. Only the seed that is sown will multiply. Unless it leaves your hand, it cannot take root and grow. If the farmer fails to plant his seed it will rot, and the life that is in the seed will die.

> *What you have today is your future in seed form, and what you do with what you have today will determine your tomorrow.*

Like wheat and other agricultural products, money and other material items can also be seeds that can be sown. In financial terms, this is called investing. The amount of financial "seed" that we reserve from the harvest for sowing determines the next harvest. A piece of money in my hand is a piece of money. If I spend the entire amount, it is eliminated and becomes useless to anyone. But if I sow it (invest it), it will grow and compound and produce not only provision for me and everyone under my care, but also more seed to be re-sown.

> *The amount of financial "seed" that we reserve from the harvest for sowing determines the next harvest.*

If you sow a small amount of money, you will receive the reward worthy of that investment. If you sow a larger amount of money, you will likewise receive the reward of that seed sown. The more seed you sow, the greater the harvest will be, with even more seeds to sow. Remember that seeds produce seeds of the same kind. If you sow a small amount, you will receive a small harvest. If you keep it in your pocket, you will get nothing.

This idea of investing for a future harvest is like the old truism, "Give a man a fish and you feed him for a day; teach a man to fish and you feed him for a lifetime." It is easy simply to give a hungry man money for a meal, but it doesn't last. He may be satisfied for a few hours, but then he will be hungry again. It is much harder to teach a hungry man to fend for himself because it requires an investment of time and energy. But it is an investment that will produce dividends for a lifetime.

Sowing our seed is not always easy. Everyone has seed of some kind, but many people never do anything with their seed. One reason is that sowing seed can be hard. There are at least three requirements for successful sowing, which many people lack.

First of all, sowing seed requires faith. It requires confidence that the time and labor we expend in sowing our seed is worthwhile because in time the seed will grow and produce an abundant harvest. In other words, we must have faith that our investment in sowing will bring in multiplied returns.

Second, sowing seed takes cooperation. There are many people who never sow any seed and yet somehow expect a harvest. Sowing is a cooperative effort. Just as a farmer's seed in a field needs the cooperation of sunshine, rain, and nutrients in the soil to transform it into a profitable, harvestable crop, so do we also need to carefully plan and thoroughly prepare when managing our financial seed.

Third, sowing seed takes vision. Some do not sow because they lack vision. They cannot see beyond the present. Five years from now their situation will still look like it does today. That weedy garden still won't have flowers in it. Nothing will have changed.

If, however, you are a planter with vision, you will take a lesson from the farmer, who sows according to his need. If he needs a lot, he sows a lot. If he needs wheat, he doesn't sow oats.

Reaping

Reaping is proportional to sowing. The more you sow, the more new seed you will have after the harvest. And the more carefully and thoroughly you sow, the easier and more abundant will be the reaping. Nevertheless, even with good sowing, the reaping will not come automatically. At least two factors are critical for reaping a good harvest.

The first factor is wisdom. You need to know how to take care of your harvest. Many people who achieve initial financial success squander it quickly through unwise spending on such objects as boats, cars, and vacation homes. Their seed money quickly becomes tied up in gadgets and things that have no lasting value. These items are not necessarily wrong in themselves; however, they do require time and money to maintain. Too often people make the mistake of not taking into account the ongoing cost of maintaining an expensive "toy" or commodity or property before buying it. Furthermore, when such things wear out, they leave no harvest behind for anyone else to reap. The money spent on them that could have been used to invest in the future is gone forever.

> *Hoarded wealth never grows and it never benefits anybody, not even the one who possesses it.*

Secondly, successful reaping involves sharing. What do you do if your harvest brings in more than you need? Hoard it? Invest it? Give it away? Hoarded wealth never grows and it never benefits anybody, not even the one who possesses it. In fact, hoarded wealth actually possesses the hoarder, not the other way around, because his heart is in bondage to his greed.

> *The best use we can make of our excess— that abundance over and above what is required for our needs—is to give it and invest it for the good of others in need.*

Your heart is the place from which you give your finances. What you spend your money on reveals what your heart is connected to. Unfortunately, many people waste their seed by giving it out everywhere except where they should be giving it. The best use we can make of our excess—that abundance over and above what is required for our needs—is to give it and invest it for the good of others in need. One life of liberality can bless many people across multiple generations.

One key principle to remember with any harvest is that some of it is for seed, and some of it is for bread. In other words, some is for sowing or investing, and some for eating or spending. We use some of our substance to nourish ourselves and maintain our own stability. This is both necessary and right. But if we unwisely consume all our harvest, we will have nothing left either to help the needy or to sow for a future harvest. We must be careful not only in how much we consume, but also in the amount and manner in which we give to others. If we give money (our seed) to the

> *One key principle to remember with any harvest is that some of it is for seed, and some of it is for bread. In other words, some is for sowing or investing, and some for eating or spending.*

poor, they'll often do something they shouldn't—they'll spend it, not sow it. It is better to give them food to eat and clothing to wear. We should take that which is in our house, that which we have, and give to our needy neighbors; but our seed should be sown in areas where we will reap a harvest.

Sowing—A Life-and-Death Decision

We can choose how and where to sow the seed we have. We can either sow to our own needs and desires alone, or to the needs and benefit of others as well. In this regard, sowing becomes, in a manner of speaking, a life-and-death decision. Although you may invest your finances wisely, if you choose to sow only to yourself, with no thought for others, you may become rich in external things yet be poor in character and in your inner self. Sowing to ourselves is like sowing to death. There are many, many people who have great material wealth but are barren and empty inside because they want to keep it all to themselves. They learn belatedly, if at all, that selfishness never satisfies.

Or we can hoard our seed, refusing to invest it, which is like standing in the middle of a field with seed in our hand yet refusing to plant it, while at the same time expecting an increase. It will never happen. Our finances will never increase as long as they remain in our hands. In this case, rather than investing for the future, we expend our resources to meet our own immediate needs, leaving nothing to fall back on. We consume our wages in the acquisition of creature comforts, most of which are beyond our means. We choose to feel good now and to please our fleshly desires now rather than save and invest our seed. In so doing, we forfeit our future, which is also tantamount to death.

Some people struggle in major battles with their finances. No matter what they do they cannot get ahead or even catch up, for that matter. They work hard to bring home a paycheck but still never have enough finances to meet their expenses. The problem is that they are consuming all their seed instead of holding some in reserve to sow into the field again. If nothing is sown, nothing can be harvested. Then your tomorrow will look the same as your today and you will never get ahead.

Investing your seed, on the other hand, is sowing to life. Anything that is living grows. If it stops growing, it starts dying. Ultimately, the only way we can grow, financially or otherwise, is by learning to look beyond ourselves and our own needs and invest in the needs and the good of others.

As was mentioned earlier in this chapter, and bears repeating, sowing to life requires vision—the ability to see past our own little world and to catch a glimpse of the world beyond, realizing that we have the power and the opportunity to make a difference in that greater world with the seed that is in our hand.

If a farmer gathers his seed and stores it for himself, it will eventually rot because there is no life to it. It can have life only when he puts it back in the ground. If he does not

> *Sowing to life requires vision…realizing that we have the power and the opportunity to make a difference in the greater world with the seed that is in our hand.*

re-sow the seed, there will be no harvest next year. But when the farmer scatters the seed onto the prepared soil, he dreams of the crop he will gather in the future. Vision means making present sacrifices and investments, and foregoing short-term gains in exchange for greater, wider, and more abundant returns in the future—over the long term.

> *Vision means making present sacrifices and investments, and foregoing short-term gains in exchange for greater, wider, and more abundant returns in the future.*

You must have faith and be willing to risk your seed in confident hope of a great harvest to come. In this sense, anything you sow, you sow in faith. A farmer goes out to sow because he sees the harvest ahead. He does not know how his seed grows, only that it does grow. In faith he prepares the soil and releases his seed into it.

When you sow in faith, envisioning the harvest, you also sow in hope—the confident expectation that your investment has not been wasted but will bring an abundant return.

The Satisfaction of Waiting

It takes time to reap a harvest. You cannot plant and then expect to see a crop pop up through the surface of the ground in a minute or an hour. The ground will give you a harvest, but it will take time. In that time you must pull the weeds of selfish ambition and keep the vermin away that will eat your seed before it has a chance to germinate. After you have sown, you need to walk in faith and anticipation that the harvest you envision will come in due time.

> *It takes time to reap a harvest.*

My wife and I enjoyed seeing our little farm grow and produce crop after crop. There is something deeply satisfying about seeing the investment of your time, seed, and labor pay off in a harvest that not only enriches you but enables you to share generously with others.

Because you brought nothing into this world and will take nothing out, every resource you have in this life you possess in trust. The difference you make in your world while on this earth will depend on how you use what you have. So the decision is yours. Will you consume your substance on your own selfish needs and desires, passing through the river of life without leaving even a ripple to show you were here, or will you aspire to greater things, embrace a higher vision, and invest your resources for the greater good of your fellowman, both now and in future generations?

FAMILY FINANCES

CHAPTER FOUR

Financial trouble is one of the leading causes of turmoil and distress in families. The mishandling of family finances often leads to division, anger, bitterness, resentment, and is a continual spark for strife as well as arguing between spouses. It can even lead to marital breakup. In fact, money-related problems are a significant factor in one out of every three broken homes. The negative impact on spouses, children, and greater society in general is both real and significant.

Potential Problems

One of the secrets to avoiding financial distress is to identify potential problem areas so they can be prevented, or eliminated if they are already present. You have to identify the problem before you can find a solution. Following are six common factors that lead to financial problems in a family.

Lack of Communication

Failure to communicate, especially about money, is a major cause of marital strife. I have heard many couples say, "We can get along fine as long as we don't talk about money, but the moment we start talking about money, all hell breaks loose!"

Why do so many married couples avoid talking about money? There could be any number of reasons, but most of them are related to fear. One of the big ones is the fear of confrontation. Very few couples like to argue, and once they discover that talking about finances means a likely disagreement, they learn to clam up, hoping to keep the peace. However, ignored problems rarely go away on their own; they just get worse.

Another fear related to talking about money is the fear of correction. Nobody likes to be told that their spending habits are wrong. Even if we sense that we're not doing things right financially, we often try to ignore the problem because we really don't want to change.

This brings us to the next reason that keeps couples from talking finances: the fear of facing reality. Many couples prefer to live in a fantasy world with regard to their finances, where they can do as they please and spend as they wish, believing that somehow everything will work itself out. It seems easier to ignore the nagging suspicion that things are not well than to face the truth head-on and deal with it.

Finally, many couples fail to talk about their finances because they are afraid of losing control. This is another fantasy. The only way to be in control financially is to be up-front, open, and fully knowledgeable at all times about where you are financially: debts, obligations, expenses, assets, liabilities.

> *The only way to be in control financially is to be up-front, open, and fully knowledgeable at all times about where you are financially: debts, obligations, expenses, assets, liabilities.*

Lack of knowledge puts you at the mercy of your finances—and of the inevitably poor decisions that result from your ignorance.

His Money, Her Money

Another common cause of financial strife in a marriage stems from many couples' practice of keeping their money separate. Instead of pooling their resources into a common "pot" designated "our" money, they maintain separate accounts of "mine" and "yours." This division easily results in conflicts over who pays for what bills, which can make budgeting and planning very difficult. Aside from that, maintaining separate accounts hinders couples from developing the sense of intimacy and oneness that is so essential for marital success and happiness.

For all couples, the ideal situation is joint money. All money belongs to both partners and all checking and savings accounts are joint accounts. This protects both partners from the selfish attitude of "That's my money. I can spend it any way I want to." Joint sharing of money fosters healthy communication, encourages mutual financial awareness, and promotes joint decision making.

Living Beyond Your Means

Many people want to appear as having lots of money to spend, even if they don't. "Keeping up with your neighbors" is a popular game in most societies. Adding to the problem is the credit-driven nature of international economies, which encourages people to spend money they don't have. Trying to keep up with others by putting on a show of wealth while living on credit is a short track to financial ruin. "Easy" credit makes it easy for couples to deceive themselves into thinking they are richer than they are. It is easy to spend assets you never see—until the bill comes due.

It is no coincidence that most financially-strapped, debt-ridden people also have no functioning household budget. Not only do they spend more than they make, but they usually have no clear idea of where their money is going or how quickly it is being consumed. What's the answer? Families need to conduct a realistic assessment of their needs and wants to determine what is really important to them and what they can afford without incurring debt. Debt is the real killer. As long as debt is in the picture, it is virtually impossible to develop financial stability and prosperity. An ancient proverb says that the rich rule over the poor and that the borrower is servant to the lender. These timeless words of wisdom are just as true today as they ever were, especially when it comes to debt.

The "Little" Things

Buying little things here and there can lead to big financial problems if a family is not careful. This is a deceptively easy way to break any budget, because when you spend or charge a little here and a little there, after a short time you realize you're broke. Rarely do people get deeply into debt all at once; it usually happens gradually. That is why debt is such a danger-ous trap.

> *Debt is such a dangerous trap... because it usually happens gradually.*

A very rich couple I know was forced to mortgage their home to pay off credit cards. They both made plenty of money, but unplanned spending ruined their financial estate. It is the little things over a period of time that add up. One day you wake up and have to mortgage your home because of all the "little things" you bought that you cannot even remember buying and might not even have anymore. Learn to save small coins! Individually, they might not be worth much, but collectively they add up. Every little bit will make a difference over the long run.

Insufficient Income

Not making enough money to make ends meet is always a major cause of stress in a family. Couples should always try their best to earn enough to meet at least their basic needs. If you have tried this and simply cannot make it on your current income, you may need to consult a professional financial counselor to help you determine a course of action. You might also consider pursuing new job skills training so you can qualify for a better-paying job.

One word of caution, however: make sure that insufficient income is really the problem. Most of the time, when families experience financial troubles, the problem is not insufficient income, but out-of-control spending. Absence of a budget and lack of discipline result in many unnecessary purchases. Creating a budget, establishing financial priorities, and imposing discipline on spending will often alleviate much of the financial problem without the need for increasing income.

> *Most of the time, when families experience financial troubles, the problem is not insufficient income, but out-of-control spending.*

"Good Deals"

Many people are going broke on "good deals." This advertising ploy entices and motivates us to overspend, especially in the areas of hobbies, habits, and recreation. Often we spend a lot of money on good deals that turn out to be not what they seem, leading us to spend more money to get what we thought we were getting in the first place!

Bulk-buying can lure us into the trap of buying more than we need. These types of businesses offer similar temptations to buy something—anything—"for less," "just in case I need it someday."

Take time to ask yourself, "Can I really afford this type of spending, not only in regard to my money, but in my time used? Would my time and money be better spent elsewhere? Are there other expenditures or investments that have a higher priority?"

Too often, "good deal" buying just leads to more financial

worry, which in turn further enflames an already smoldering financial crisis.

Seven Tips for Avoiding Financial Problems

Be in Agreement

Before making any major purchase or spending a large amount of money, make sure you and your spouse are in agreement on the purchase.

Also, take time beforehand, in a peaceful moment, to define what constitutes a "large amount of money" so that there is no confusion!

Allow your partner, who may not always be in full agreement with your plans, to serve as a check and balance for you. What seems like a good idea to you may not be actually in your best interest, and you may need the different perspective of your partner to help you realize it. Talking things over first allows you to obtain input from your partner. It may shed a different light on your original plan. Don't be too proud to listen to or follow your spouse's advice.

> *Allow your partner, who may not always be in full agreement with your plans, to serve as a check and balance for you.*

Get Counseling From Others

Listen to good counsel. Humility is essential here, along with a genuinely teachable spirit. Search for someone whose judgment you trust and who you know will be honest with you and tell you what you need to hear, not what you want to hear. Expect a word of warning here. Rarely are we happy to hear warnings. Usually we resist them, deny them, or in some other way react negatively to them. They may challenge us to make changes we don't want to make. However, if we will listen to a warning and ponder it, we are more likely to prosper and succeed.

Don't Make Hasty Decisions

Always allow at least 24 hours to pass before making the decision to purchase anything that is not in the budget. Talk about it together, think about it, and then sleep on it. This will help forestall a hasty decision you might later regret.

In many cases, you might want to put the decision on hold for as long as a month. Say, for instance, I want an item that I see on June 1. What I often do is put it on hold until June 30 and then ask, "Do I still really want that, or have I lost interest in it?" Was it just an impulse? Many times by the end of the month, I don't even want that item any longer. Because most of the purchases that get us in trouble are impulse purchases, this discipline of waiting a month will save you a lot of money. An impulse never lasts a month.

Know the Impact of Your Decisions

You should understand the impact of your decisions. There are no independent decisions. Every one of our decisions limits or creates other opportunities in our lives. A certain amount of finances will flow into your life. What you do with what you receive will determine your future. Every decision you make has both long-term and short-term effects—positive or negative—on you, your family, your friends, your business, and your associates.

Ask yourself, "Is this thing a need or a want?" Find out, for instance, before you buy, how purchasing a new camera or television is going to affect your finances. Don't spend your money blindly or hastily.

Set Financial Goals

Setting financial goals will help you prepare for the future. For example, if in ten years you would like to have a certain amount of money saved to send your child to college, you need to plan now how much you should set aside to help you achieve this goal. A financial counselor can help you make this decision and assist you in setting up a reasonable and practical plan.

Some common financial goals for which you may want to establish planning strategies include:

- **Achieving financial freedom in a given number of years.**
- **Getting out of debt.**
- **Sending your children to college.**
- **Buying a home.**
- **Starting a family business.**

None of these will happen accidentally; achieving them requires deliberate planning. In setting your financial goals, you must have a written plan that includes where you are going and how you are going to get there. Your financial plan is like your road map; you must follow it if you hope to reach your destination.

> *In setting your financial goals, you must have a written plan that includes where you are going and how you are going to get there.*

Invest Your Resources

Invest so that you will be able to help financially not only your future prosperity but also that of your children and grandchildren. Research worthy causes that you believe in and invest in those as you have the means. Commit a portion of your substance to the betterment of other people and the planet. Use your natural talents and abilities to better yourself in the job market. You are your own best resource. Funds carefully spent on improving skills and knowledge can certainly give you a good return for your money. An experienced financial counselor can help you find the right places for your money.

Budget Your Money

Budgeting is simply planning ahead. It is a guideline that helps you determine how to use and invest your money wisely. A good budget will reflect your goals and priorities in life. For this reason, every family's budget will be different, even among families with similar income levels and financial and social backgrounds. There

> **Budgeting is simply planning ahead.**

is no single "right" budget. Whatever budget establishes your family on a solid financial foundation and reflects your family goals and priorities in life is the right budget for you.

A budget makes you aware of where your money has gone or is going to go. It helps you make better financial decisions. A good budget will also help you cut down on your unnecessary spending so that you can live within your means. Living on a budget helps you keep your vision and plans in focus, enabling you to face tomorrow with complete confidence.

A good budget will help you discover problem areas and make it easier to correct them. Having a budget in place will help forestall panic and hasty decisions, especially when an emergency arises. Instead of fear, you will have peace of mind, and wisdom to deal with the problem. When you have a sound budget in place, a large number of decisions have already been made about your money in advance. That way, you don't have to keep on deciding how to spend your money every time you get your paycheck. You already know what you're going to do

> **When you have a sound budget in place, a large number of decisions have already been made about your money in advance.**

with the money, and can move ahead with confidence that you will have more than enough money to meet your needs.

How to Develop a Budget

The first step in developing a sound, workable budget is to gain a clear and thorough knowledge of what your income is and what other resources are available to you. Examine your financial records carefully—forms that indicate how much money you have earned, saved, invested, paid to the government, etc. Make sure you are not omitting any financial assets you have.

Second, list all your monthly living expenses. These include such things as:

- **Food—at home and away from home.**
- **Supplies.**
- **Household services—baby sitters, house care, etc.**
- **Vehicle maintenance and transportation.**
- **Personal care and clothing.**
- **Entertainment.**
- **Medical expenses and medicines.**

Third, list all your fixed expenses. Fixed expenses include, in part:

- **Insurance.**
- **Utilities.**
- **Vehicle or house payments.**
- **Taxes.**
- **Gifts/giving.**
- **Other.**

Try to spread the payment of your larger expenses evenly so

that they are not all due at the same time. If your insurance bill, for example, is paid quarterly, divide the quarterly total by three and set that amount aside each month. When it's time to pay, it won't take such a big bite out of one paycheck.

Next, in your planning, include unexpected expenses such as vehicle repairs or doctor bills. It will help if you start an emergency fund to handle such matters. A good rule of thumb for an emergency fund is to keep on hand an amount equivalent to four-to-eight months' living expenses. If that is too much for you to set aside at one time, work up to it as you can. It is important to take positive action now.

Fifth, make your budget simple to follow, realistic, and adjustable in case of emergencies. Don't make your budget any more complex than necessary to meet your needs. The simpler the better.

Sixth, never think of your household budget as a weapon with which to attack your spouse's spending habits. Otherwise, your marriage will become a battleground.

Finally, make sure your budget is realistic. The fastest way to feel discouraged and defeated is to set up an unrealistic budget. Don't try to break all your bad spending habits at once. Success takes time, effort, and patience. Tackle one or two trouble spots at a time. Even a little progress will encourage you to keep going.

Teach Your Children

Family finances involve the children too. As parents, we have the responsibility to teach our children to be wise financial managers even while they are still children. Here are three basic principles you should teach your children about finances:

1. **How to save and prepare for future needs.**

2. **How to work and earn money.**

3. **How to budget and spend wisely.**

In our family, our children had to work for their money; we didn't just give it to them. We taught them that there is a reward for working. When each of our children reached the age of 13, we started giving them an allowance which was enough to cover all their personal needs. Each one was responsible for budgeting his or her own money and making decisions about how to use it. Envelopes with labels—"savings," "giving," "clothes," "recreation," and so forth—was one way they could choose to organize their money. If he or she failed to plan wisely and consequently needed money, we did not bail him or her out with a loan. Our children knew they had to learn to manage their finances according to wise and sound guidelines and principles.

Today, there is a debt mentality prevalent in our society. Parents and families who know nothing about managing finances are not able to teach their children the wise use of money. This fosters a deepening spiral of credit cards, loans, debt, and financial failure from one generation to another. But when we begin to learn and apply wise and time-tested principles of finance, being careful to train our children likewise, then we will be laying a solid foundation for a prosperous and successful future.

THE DEBT TRAP

Debt is the number-one cause of financial misery and bond-age. If you are one of the few who are debt-free, consider yourself fortunate indeed and determine within yourself to do whatever you need to do to stay that way. If, however, you are one of the many for whom debt is a fact of life, let me assure you that there is hope. The way out of debt begins by waking up to a few sobering realities. Remember, you have to recognize the problem before you can solve it.

As long as you remain in debt, you will never be financially free or prosperous. Debt will continue to be your master. It will maintain control over you because you will need to expend all your labor working to pay it off. Financial freedom will remain nonex-istent because your creditors will continue to determine how you use your money. In other words, no matter how much money you make, if you are in debt, you are not truly free to use your money as you wish. You are in bond-age to your creditors' payment

> **No matter how much money you make, if you are in debt, you are not truly free to use your money as you wish.**

41

schedules. Your creditors have the most important say in your financial decisions; after all, it is their money. In addition, interest rates ensure that you end up, in the long run, paying much more money than the value of whatever caused you to go into debt. Debt also strips you of financial privacy. For all these reasons, you should at all costs avoid incurring debt—or determine to get out of debt as quickly as possible.

Indebtedness often represents a lack of self-control. It is largely the result of a failure to rule over our indulgent desires, and instead, gives free reign to our five senses.

> *Indebtedness often represents a lack of self-control.*

Make no mistake about it—undisciplined responses to daily stimuli, impulses, and desires can keep you broke. They can also destroy your life. Lack of self-discipline reveals itself in virtually every area of life. Indebtedness is just one symptom. If you are in debt because of failure to control your money, examine your life closely and you will probably discover other areas where your life is out of control. Let me share with you an example from my personal experience.

The First Rule of Holes

A man once came to me seeking some financial counseling. He was earning $200,000 a year, yet was totally broke. Confused and desperate, he wanted me to help him figure out what was wrong. It didn't make sense that he could be in such a poor situation financially with such a large amount of money coming into his house. As we talked together, a picture began to emerge that explained the man's problem.

Although this man had an impressive income, he had an even more excessive lifestyle. Money was going out as fast as it came in. Everything that was coming in was immediately going back out to pay bills that he had created. Bringing his paycheck home was like throwing gasoline onto a fire—it was just consumed. Far from creating wealth and a future for his children, this man was digging a huge hole.

As my friend's lifestyle began to unfold, we found that the numbers didn't add up. For example, this man had two children on which he would typically spend $37,000 on gifts yearly. A family living in a developing nation could eat for several months with what it cost him just to buy the cases of batteries to keep all the toys running! This man had the best of everything—Cadillacs, Corvettes, and condos—yet he failed to see where the money was hemorrhaging from his bank account. The problem and the solution were both obvious. This man had dug himself into a hole. And the first rule of holes is…when you are in one, stop digging.

There are many who dig themselves into holes, financial and otherwise. To the outside world, these people look successful with heaps of money and material possessions flowing through their hands and taking up space in their driveways. Riches can be likened to the piles of dirt mounding up around the hole being dug. Everyone else sees the pile of treasure, but the one digging the hole is nowhere to be seen. Why? Because he or she is at the bottom of the hole…of debt! Until they recognize the problem and take concrete steps to solve it, people in this situation continue to dig deeper and deeper holes not only for themselves, but for their children as well. They live in the hole, and they will raise their children in the hole. Consequently, the only inheritance they leave to any future generation is a shovel.

Digging the Hole

How is it that some of us find ourselves digging holes? To begin with, we live in a world whose monetary and financial systems are built on things of no value. The money that moves from hand to hand is little more than paper. The same is true of the stock market and especially the e-stocks, which are basically thin air. We trade them back and forth like a game that never declares a winner.

There is no real substance to most of what we buy and sell. Yet with those material things, we dig deeper holes for ourselves where there is no bottom in sight. Greed and fear drive us. We try in desperation to get as much as we can any way we can get it, and we live in fear that someone else's pile, at the rim of the hole he is digging, is becoming bigger than our own.

How do you know if you are digging a hole for yourself? Check your credit card balances. Do you pay each debt in full at the end of the month, or do you leave a balance? Do you ever get a little knot in your stomach when you hand that card to the waitress or cashier at a restaurant, wondering whether you have gone over your credit limit? To be sure, credit cards are good and convenient tools when used wisely. But if you always maintain a balance, all you do is throw your treasure into the incinerator, where you will never get it back.

Another way of knowing if you are digging yourself into a hole is to examine your attitude. Do you live with a sense of entitlement? Do you believe you deserve that new car that carries a payment you cannot afford? Are you driving to a vacation home hoping that the telephone and electric companies won't disconnect you while you are away?

You can know you are digging a hole when you look at what is piling up in your life around you. Are there lots of things that you thought you could not live without, yet they are hidden away in storage? Are you still paying off last year's holiday bills a year later, just in time to add new bills to the pile? That pile of stuff is like the dirt collecting around the rim of the hole you are digging for yourself. You are lost and hidden behind all your "stuff."

Indeed, through self indulgence, you may be one of the many people who have simultaneously piled up "stuff" as well as significant debt, and thereby forfeited your financial future in exchange for instant gratification right now. Like a child whining and begging for candy in a grocery store, your immature spirit is unwilling to wait for what you desire. You want what you want right now, no matter what you have to do to get it. And if you manage to get it, you usually end up regretting it later.

This hole of debt also prevents you from realizing

> *Through self indulgence, many people have simultaneously piled up "stuff" as well as significant debt, and thereby forfeited their financial future in exchange for instant gratification right now.*

your fullest potential in life. Debt robs you of both resources and time. You end up giving the best years of your life to a stranger and building empires for other people, corporations, and finance companies. Your own labor should make you wealthy, not someone else.

At the same time, you must be careful not to fall into the trap of pursuing wealth simply for its own sake. Such an empty pursuit

> *The gaining of wealth as an end in itself is a very poor investment of a life. Wealth for its own sake never brings happiness, contentment, or satisfaction.*

is just as dangerous to inner health and welfare as being in bondage to debt—probably more so. The gaining of wealth as an end in itself is a very poor investment of a life. Wealth for its own sake never brings happiness, contentment, or satisfaction.

The wisdom and experience of centuries continually affirms that there is no correlation between wealth and happiness. There is, however, a correlation between financial bondage and unhappiness. Money cannot buy happiness, but the constant stress and struggle over bills you can't afford to pay can steal it from you.

The Bondage of Debt

To be in debt is to be chained in bondage to law. Debt is a weight that hangs around and over us, constricting and compromising our lives and our financial freedom. In the old days, when a person's debt was more than his income, he was thrown into prison. Although there might not be debtors' prisons today, per se, we still most certainly remain in bondage to those we owe.

The debtors' prisons of today are housed in bigger and fancier buildings—banks and credit card companies. They greet us at their entrances with smiling faces as we walk through the doors of their impressive granite and glass offices. The folks inside seem so nice, so harmless as they offer to stretch our paychecks into boats and vacation homes and the latest model cars. They make it especially easy for us today, not wasting our time because we often never have to personally visit them. They send us a colorful little brochure or a "pre-approved" offer before they drag us into "jail." The buildings don't look much like prisons, but these credit companies hold us and our destinies captive just as surely as if they have clapped us in chains.

Debt also functions like an addiction. Addictions lure us into a feeling of control of our lives somehow, and those free credit card offers we get in the mail are like free samples given out by a drug dealer. We feel we must have some kind of material fix to stay comfortable. Our addiction to possessing things results in debt that destroys us as surely as heroin or crack.

The means by which we get into debt vary from credit cards to car payments. Some people take out second mortgages to finance the "toys" they think they need in order to keep up with the neighbors. It is so easy—too easy—to get credit cards today, which are the primary cause of bankruptcy. According to the American Bankruptcy Institute, more than 90 percent of personal bankruptcies in the United States are due to credit card debt. Whatever the means, the result is ruinous.

In addition to being considered bondage and an addiction, indebtedness carries with it certain consequences that are often unanticipated because they have no direct connection to money. Debt is a merciless thief that steals some of the most valuable aspects of our lives.

Debt Steals Your Future

Debt robs the future to satisfy the present. Every time you borrow, you take future earnings, time, and energy and spend them on the present. Whenever you go into debt, you sacrifice your future and your children's futures on the altars of pleasure and appearance. You cannot afford to send your kids to college because you are over your head in debt. When you continually live beyond your means, you consequently strip yourself of blessing and provision.

> **Debt robs the future to satisfy the present.**

When you pile up consumer debt, you mortgage your future. You commit future earnings to pay for present desires. You go to work on Monday to make sure the bills are paid on Friday. Hence, you have become a slave.

Many times we use credit cards on impulse. Something catches our eye and hooks our heart, and we pull out the credit card and throw it down on the counter or the desk. Beware—decisions made in a moment take a long time to repay.

Debt Steals Your Freedom

When you borrow money, you bring the banker into your home. He tracks all over your carpets and there is nothing you can do about it. He puts his feet up on your furniture and laughs, waiting like a vulture for you to run out of breath. He gets rich while you pay him interest, and he will gladly take back the furniture when

47

you can no longer make the payments.

It doesn't stop there. What about the car you borrowed money for in order to drive? Not only do you get the car, but you get the banker to ride along in the backseat. Then when you miss a payment, you end up riding in the backseat while the banker takes over driving the car.

When you incur debt, you enter into a relationship of servitude. This servitude severely restricts your freedom to live life on your own terms: to take off work whenever you need to, to travel when you want, to spend time with your family, or to fulfill your personal dreams and goals. You are so busy slaving away to pay the bills that your own dreams have to be put on hold indefinitely. No matter how hard you try, you never seem to get to the end of the payments. There is always another payment and then another payment on top of that one. It never seems to end…and that is just the way credit is designed. Why do you

> *When you incur debt, you enter into a relationship of servitude.*

think credit card companies can afford to lend so much money? Because they have tens of thousands of consumers strung out for decades trying to pay off their balances at exorbitant interest rates through minimum payments each month.

With debt, a decision made in a moment can lead to many long years of repayment—and regret. And in the end what do you have to show for it? Years off your productive life and a worn-out

> *With debt, a decision made in a moment can lead to many long years of repayment and regret.*

or obsolete item worth only a fraction of what you paid.

Add to this the fact that, today, credit is more readily available than ever before and debt becomes an even greater danger. Many people who normally would not qualify for credit can now get cars, furniture, electronic equipment, credit cards, houses, boats, and more. There is a reason they would not normally qualify: insufficient income or insufficient assets that render them a high-default risk. Yet, lower standards in recent years have allowed many non-credit-worthy people to get credit. These lower standards—and the resultant significant rise in payment defaults—are a major factor in the current economic difficulties we are experiencing in our nation today.

A couple generations ago, people saved their money for what they wanted, and then purchased it from their savings. The current trend is to buy with credit rather than savings, because credit is fast, easy, and painless (at least until the payments mount up). There is no waiting. Another reason why fewer people purchase using their savings is because fewer people have savings. Many people are so deeply in debt that they cannot afford to build up any savings; they simply don't have the money. And the easy availability of credit has created the false assumption in the minds of many that savings are no longer necessary. Why save when you can borrow? This is a mind-set that can (and does) lead to financial disaster.

As long as you are willing to mortgage the future to live better today, your best labor, talent, and wealth-creating capability will flow into another man's pockets. Your boss may pay you a "fair" wage, but your greatest profitability and industry will stay with him. He will benefit many times over because of your servitude. Wouldn't it be better to free yourself so that your labor, talent, and industry can enrich your family and enable you to bless others rather than line another man's pockets with wealth for 30 or 40 years and have nothing to show for it at the end except a barely adequate pension (if that)?

When you live and work to pay off debt, you give your years to those who don't care about you, and others are filled with your wealth. This is not their fault; it's yours. You have given them the power over you when you had to have that large screen TV or vacation rental. In the end you will end up broke, spending many more times the original amount than if you had just paid cash, but instead you pay a huge amount of interest. Credit card interest is obscene, as much as 25 percent. When you borrow from tomorrow to spend today, you lose control over your future.

Any way you look at it, debt is a trap that can keep you in bondage for years.

Debt Steals Your Harvest

When you enter into debt, you turn the season of your life upside down. Instead, you should be sowing seed, watering, cultivating, and expecting a harvest. But unfortunately, you take the little seed that you have, and either eat it or surrender it to others so they can plant it. In other words, you violate the "Law of the Seasons." Seasons are part of the natural cycle of life, and there is an appointed season for everything.

Seasons regulate the growth and nurturing of all life on our planet, a recurring cycle of seedtime and harvest. Violation of this cycle always leads to problems. Seedtime must precede the harvest or there will be no harvest. And each must be done in its proper season. A farmer who waits until summer to plant his seed will never reap a harvest. The quality of the harvest depends also on the quality of the soil in which the seed is planted. While a seed will always contain life, it is where the seed goes that makes the difference.

There are four steps to a harvest: preparation of the soil, seedtime, watering, and harvest. If you do not understand these four seasons, you will end up in trouble. This is true in every area of life, not just agriculture. It is especially true with regard to finances, credit, and debt. Credit and debt ignore the soil preparation and watering stages, reducing the process to seedtime (having funds available) and harvest (get product). Our greed and impatient desire drive us to speed up the process. We want what we want right now, whether we can afford it or not, so we use credit to get it, and end up in debt. The Law of the Seasons is turned completely upside down. Anything worth having is worth preparing for and waiting for. Even good things can be bad for us if we try to acquire them "out of season." There is a season for everything, and we must learn to wait patiently for that season, using the time in between to get ready for the harvest.

When a farmer sows a seed, he doesn't go out every day and pull back the soil to see if the seed is growing. It has to have time to grow. Likewise, you can't sow your seed and seek an immediate harvest. You must be patient

> *Anything worth having is worth preparing for and waiting for. Even good things can be bad for us if we try to acquire them "out of season."*

through the winter season when there seems to be nothing happening. Farmers don't take naps in the winter, but neither do they stand over the planted seed waiting for it to pop up out of the ground. It is a matter of faith—doing our part and trusting nature to take its course.

We observe the season and understand that there are going to be perceived high times and low times—times when we bring a crop to market and times when we spread manure. Both are necessary though the fragrance isn't the same. The lesson is— when things are going well, don't go out and buy a new car. Wait for the harvest. Buying a new car may be fun and seem like the right thing to do—until the coupon book comes in the mail. You have committed a significant portion of your harvest to someone who invested nothing in its planting and cultivation.

You must grow with the season. If abundance comes, store some away for the dry times. If you hit a low point, don't panic and sell the farm. Pull out that which you've saved; keep the trend going. However, many people's harvest must be spent to pay for their borrowed seed. Living in debt—borrowing against your harvest—becomes a cycle. You live today and pay tomorrow.

When you acquire debt, you must live from paycheck to paycheck and hope not to get too many calls from creditors in between. The entire focus of your life is now fixed on paying your bills, not on enjoying the fruits of your labor. And that is certainly no way to live.

Debt Steals Your Focus and Creativity

Another practical consequence of debt is that it will change your focus. Instead of looking for and seizing opportunities for growth and advancement, you will be too busy focusing on paying your bills. A heavy debt burden can create a very negative mind-set that is tough to overcome. I once heard of a man who taped his overdue bills to his mirror in order to keep them in the front of his mind. His intentions may have been good, but he inadvertently set himself up for failure by focusing on the negative.

You cannot motivate yourself with negatives. You will start to feel buried, seeing no way out of your predicament. Obsessive focusing on your problems will either blind you to opportunities for positive change, or discourage you with the realization that you cannot take advantage of any opportunities you do see. Debt limits your creativity; you can no longer think big. It causes you to live too close to the edge. And if you live too close to the edge, you will eventually slip and fall.

> *Debt limits your creativity; you can no longer think big. It causes you to live too close to the edge.*

Debt Steals Your Sense of Wealth

In addition to changing your focus, borrowing creates within you a false sense of wealth. You think you can afford things because of credit available rather than because of income produced. As a result, you spend more than you make, which leads to financial distress and even bankruptcy. Credit is a particularly dangerous trap because it is so subtle and alluring. Over the short term, credit cards take away the "pain" of buying. The ready availability of credit cards and lines of credit with high credit limits make it easy to defer the day of reckoning. Just pull out the plastic and zip—you're done. Quick, easy, and painless—until the statement arrives. When you don't pay with cash, you easily lose the sense of relationship between your hard work and your spending. Thus, you spend more than you should, even more than you realize you are spending. Studies have shown that credit customers in restaurants spend as much as 100 percent more than customers who pay in cash. Shopping is even worse. For example, people who buy clothing with a credit card generally spend three times as much as those who use cash to pay for their purchases.

If you have a tendency to use your credit card for anything and everything, let me give you some advice. Before you buy on credit, restore your sense of relationship between your income and your spending by asking yourself how much your proposed purchase will really cost you. For example, suppose that the item you want to purchase costs a days' worth of your wages. Ask yourself, "Is this item really worth one full day of my labor?" If it is, buy it. If not, you may want to reconsider.

> **When you don't pay with cash, you easily lose the sense of relationship between your hard work and your spending.**

Debt Steals Your Relationships

Debt can and does destroy relationships. This is why lending to or borrowing from friends or family is rarely a good idea. If the borrower becomes servant to the lender, this means that a significant relational shift has taken place, particularly between friends or family members. Entering into a lender/borrower relationship with someone close to you will affect your relationship with that person on a social level. Suppose you borrow money from a friend to help you in your business. You have just been entrusted with a portion of his treasure, and he suddenly has a vested interest in the affair that goes beyond your friendship. Now your friend has a personal stake in your business because he has invested some of his wealth in it. He judges you on how you spend your money, what kind of car you drive, where and how long you go on vacation, et cetera .

This doesn't mean we should never lend; that's what friends are for. But it does mean that we must be careful and wise in our lending decisions, with full awareness of the potential pitfalls. One good rule of thumb is to lend only what you are willing to lose.

> *Lend only what you are willing to lose.*

Keep in mind always that lending or borrowing carries the risk of destroying relationships by opening the door for anger, resentment, estrangement, or an unforgiving spirit.

Debt Steals Your Reputation

In social or business circles—indeed, in every arena of life, there is no substitute for a good name. A good name is our greatest collateral when we want to do business. The quickest way to ruin your reputation and spoil your good name is to become known as a covenant-breaker— someone who doesn't pay his bills.

> *A good name is our greatest collateral when we want to do business.*

When you take on debt, you enter into a covenant. You take money out of the banker's pocket with the promise to repay him. Even when you hook up to the electric company, you promise to take responsibility to pay for what you use. Whatever the realm of debt you enter into, it is all based on a promise to repay, whether it is the utility company or the clothing store. When you don't repay, you waste money on penalties and interest. If you don't pay those bills on time, you have broken covenant. And who can trust a covenant-breaker? How long would you continue to trust someone who repeatedly broke his word to you?

The way we handle our debts and pay our bills reveals the true nature of our character, regardless of what we say or how we act. If you live constantly in debt and routinely fail to pay your bills, is it any wonder that people around you consider you untrustworthy?

A good name can get you money and make you money, while a bad name will keep both far away from you. Every time credit is extended to you, your credit score drops. In fact, every credit check performed on you by a creditor lowers your credit score. Every individual creditor or bank would like their debt with you to be your only debt, which is why the higher your debt in relation to your income, the less willing they are to extend additional credit to you. So, if you know that you will lower your credit score every time you use credit, make sure that the debt you incur will increase you. In other words, don't go into debt unless you can invest what you borrow in ways that will bring returns greater than the total cost of the debt, including interest. Otherwise, your indebtedness could hinder you from taking advantage of better opportunities that come along.

> *A good name can get you money and make you money, while a bad name will keep both far away from you.*

Debt Steals Your Rest

When you live under a load of debt, you are robbed of sleep. The last thing you think about before falling asleep is debt. The first thing you think about in the morning is debt. The topic of conversations with your spouse is debt. Debt—and the fear and worry that come with it—dominate your life.

Debt lies at the bottom of more marital problems and breakups than any other factor. When couples come to me for counseling, the first obstacle that usually comes up is the realm of finances. Debts both large and small have claimed hold of their budget and robbed them of rest and peace.

I have counseled very few couples whose finances are in order. To put it another way, the couples whose finances seem to be in order have fewer problems of any kind. Maybe the reason is that finances are only an indication of greater concerns and priorities. If they are at peace with themselves, each other, and the world, they need not dull pain with material possessions in order to feel better about themselves.

Debt and discouragement are all around us, ready to steal our peace. They come into our homes through TV and the Internet. They leap from the pages of fashion magazines and sale flyers inviting us to fit in with the rest of the unsettled world. The best way to preserve our rest and ensure our financial peace of mind is to avoid the debt trap. This requires constant diligence, just as a gardener must be ever watchful to keep foxes and rabbits from devouring his produce before he can bring it to harvest.

Freedom From The Trap

Chapter Six

Perhaps it is already too late to avoid the debt trap because you are already in it. Don't despair. The good news is that all the destructive effects of debt are reversible. Though debt can be a cancer, there is an effective chemotherapy that will rid your life and heart of the disease of debt. There is a way to get the banker out of your home and out of the driver's seat of your car. The only question is whether or not you are willing to take the medicine. And only you can answer that question.

With these truths in mind, let's consider some important principles for avoiding debt and digging out of the hole.

1. Live within your means.

In other words, avoid spending money you don't have. It's that simple.

> *Avoid spending money you don't have.*

2. Stop the outflow.

Place a temporary freeze on all unnecessary spending. Until you know where all your money is going, spend only on the items you absolutely need. At a minimum, your income should equal all your needed spending.

Institute a new financial principle: save first, then spend. Before spending a penny of your income, set aside a portion for savings. Even if you can save only a few dollars at a time to begin with, it is important to develop the habit. Stop telling yourself that you can't afford to save. You can't afford not to save.

> **Save first, then spend.**

3. Evaluate your cash flow.

Know where all your money is going. You can't plug a leak if you don't know where the hole is. What you are trying to accomplish here is not a budget but a spending analysis. Examine all your bills and financial records carefully. Write down every expense you can think of, even those that seem insignificant. Your goal is to account for every penny, as much as possible.

> **Account for every penny, as much as possible.**

4. Stop spending money for what isn't "bread."

Each time you take that credit card or checkbook out of your wallet and have no intention to pay the balance off at the end of the month, you are vainly attempting to find some kind of solace or peace. You are foolishly spending money on what is not "bread"— what will give you absolutely no life.

Before you buy anything, you should ask, "Is this bread life-giving to me—do I need this?" If you come to the conclusion that what you are purchasing is life-giving, then pay cash.

5. Don't buy anything on impulse.

It's a good idea to leave your checkbook or credit card in the car or at home when you are out shopping. The deal that comes along that is just too good to be true probably is. The deal of a lifetime on that shiny new SUV with the $500 monthly payment is going to be there again. That salesman who tells you that you must buy it today probably also has bills to pay at the end of the month and will extend the same or better price when you can afford it.

Most of the trouble you will find yourself in comes about in the twinkling of an eye—the twinkle of some shiny bauble that goes from your head to your heart in seconds. Never buy anything on impulse. If you have been in the place of preparation to buy something and already have funds and budget set aside to do so, then take advantage of a good opportunity when it presents itself. There is a world of difference in this situation. It is not impulse buying when you have planned for it. The question of impulse buying is really who is in control—your head or your heart. You should not spend money with your heart.

> **Never buy anything on impulse.**

6. Never buy anything with credit cards that cannot be paid off in that month.

Credit cards are a potential hazard to your financial security. Credit is not the problem, but the misuse of it can cause financial ruin. Use credit cards only for convenience. Whatever you charge on your card should already be in your budget. Here's another tip: never make only minimum payments on a credit card bill. Minimum payments are designed to take years to pay off, regardless of the beginning balance. In the end, interest alone will exceed the cost of the item or items purchased. Interest payments are how the credit card companies make money, and they total billions of dollars a year. Why give that money to a credit card company? Avoid credit and keep the money for yourself. Because this is so important, let me repeat it: Never charge anything that will not be paid off in full at the end of the month!

7. Avoid borrowing money.

Though borrowing money may sometimes be necessary, it is generally an unhealthy practice that should be avoided whenever possible. You can't borrow your way to the top or into a better position in life.

Large amounts of debt can alter people's personalities, rarely for the better. Debt can cause good employees to become desperate and resort to dishonest measures. Sleepless nights over debt are followed by poor work habits. Debt can cause chronic irritability and even ruin friendships.

Borrowing mortgages your future. Many people trade their future for present pleasures. They borrow for those things they cannot presently afford, only to find that the payments remain long after the thrill is gone. How sad! What bondage! How heavy a burden! You cannot allow the present pleasures of life and the desires of your flesh to ensnare you in future bondage. You will only end up becoming a slave to past pleasures. If you can't afford it, don't buy it!

Never borrow from friends, relatives, or family members. The inability to repay on time has destroyed even the best of relationships. Depending on the amount of debt, lifelong friends may become lifelong enemies.

> *Many people trade their future for present pleasures. They borrow for those things they cannot presently afford, only to find that the payments remain long after the thrill is gone.*

8. Budget and manage your finances.

One ancient source advises us to know the condition of our "flocks" and our "herds" so that we will not lose our estate. That which was true for an agrarian-based society long ago is just as true for our industrial and post-industrial world today. It is the people who do not watch over their estate who lose money. Some people just work, and work, and work, and work…and make money… only to lose it because they do not manage it. You need to know what you have and manage it wisely.

9. Do not co-sign for another.

Many a friendship has been destroyed because someone has co-signed on a loan for someone he knew and trusted. When you co-sign a note, you are taking full responsibility for the debt. If anything goes wrong, you will be held responsible for paying it off. What you are doing is guaranteeing something that you cannot control. That is never wise.

10. Pay off your creditors.

When you have piled-up credit debt, you should use the divide-and-conquer method of paying off your creditors. Stop spending your creditors' money and begin to pay off the debts beginning with the smallest one first. Once that is paid off, add that money to the next debt. Make sure you are making monthly payments to all to whom you owe money. Don't wait for the next threat of disconnection. The debt will be paid in due time and you will be out of the hole.

> *Use the divide-and-conquer method when paying off your creditors.*

The Right Attitude Toward Debt

Always remember that the ultimate goal is financial freedom! Everything you do must move you progressively toward that goal. But full freedom is not possible as long as you are saddled with debt. Commit yourself to becoming debt-free and start today.

> *Commit yourself to becoming debt-free and start today.*

Remember also that not all debt is bad, but it is dangerous. Before incurring debt, make sure you understand all the risks and are aware of all the possible consequences. Don't go into a debt situation blind and unprepared. Be prepared for worst-case scenarios and always have a backup plan.

Money is a tool--a means to an end. Use money; make your money work for you. Don't let money use or control you. Learn how to make banks and other lenders become vehicles of financial increase for you rather than creditors who constantly consume your assets.

If you must borrow, always borrow against something, never yourself. Don't set yourself up to become the slave of a lender. Make sure your debt is backed up by something of value that can be sold to satisfy the deficiency if necessary. Credit card companies owe their immense success in large part to the fact that the average consumer does not understand this principle. Do not put up yourself or your labor as collateral for a debt. That is nothing but slavery.

> *If you must borrow, always borrow against something, never yourself.*

Instead of a debtor, why not become a lender? What do you own or control that could be leased, rented, or sold with you as the mortgagor? Evaluate every debt and spending opportunity.

Finally, remember that with few exceptions, ownership is always better than renting or leasing. Some of those exceptions include items that are used infrequently or seasonally—items that depreciate in value quickly; wants; vacations; luxury items.

Why the Rich Are Rich, and the Poor are Poor

Chapter Seven

Ask the average man or woman on the street why the rich are rich and the poor are poor and you will get any number of answers. Some will say that the rich are rich because of greed and dishonesty, while others will attribute wealth to hard work and wise investments. The poor, on the other hand, are poor either because of oppression and exploitation or because they are lazy, unskilled, and lack a proper work ethic. Depending on the individual, any of these responses may be true.

There is, however, a deeper and more fundamental reason for the difference between rich and poor: knowledge. Generally speaking, rich people know and understand the purpose and use of money while the poor do not. One of the main reasons the rich get richer and the poor get poorer—and the middle class struggles with debt— is because the subject of how to manage (or mis-manage) money is handed down from generation to generation. Parents who have never learned the right way to manage money pass on that ignorance to their children, and the cycle of poverty and financial bondage continues for another generation.

Perhaps the biggest difference between the rich and the poor is in how they use their time. The poor spend their time working

> *The poor spend their time working for money, while the rich spend their time making money work for them.*

for money, while the rich spend their time making money work for them. It is a matter of attitude and mind-set as much as anything else.

Before we consider the differences between rich and poor in greater depth, we need to be clear on some terms. Many people, perhaps most, tend to equate one's profession with one's job or business. This is a mistake. Your profession is what you do; your business is what your money does. When talking money and finances, it is important to understand the meanings and relationships between four money terms: income, expenses, assets, and liabilities.

Income is the money you bring in from whatever source: job, investment returns, interest on savings, etc. Any money you receive that is yours to use is income.

Expenses include all the money you spend: rent or mortgage, car payments, utilities, groceries, phone bill, etc. Anything you pay out on a regular basis is an expense.

Assets are anything you possess that pays you: savings, investments, rental property, etc. Anything that makes more money than it costs you is an asset.

Liabilities are anything that costs you money in excess of what they return to you, which is often nothing: debts, perishable or depreciating items purchased on credit, etc.

> *Your profession is what you do; your business is what your money does.*

Contrary to what most people have been taught, homes can be a liability, instead of an asset, particularly if you have a high mortgage payment, or high maintenance, or both. A house is an asset only as long as you can sell it for more than what it costs you.

If you want proof that a house is a liability, just ask any of the thousands of homeowners caught in the current economic crisis with variable-rate mortgages they can no longer pay, for a house that is now worth less than they owe on it.

The Poor

The primary distinction that separates the poor, the middle class, and the rich is how they think about—and use—money. To put it another way, your attitude and use of money will largely determine which classification you fall into: poor, middle class, or rich. Certainly, income level has something to do with it, but only in relation to outgo (expenses). If your expenses equal or exceed your income, you are "poor," regardless of how much you make. If you earn a million dollars a year but your expenses are one and a half million dollars a year, you are not rich. The key is flexibility: possessing the financial resources to get what you need and do what you want whenever you desire without any outside entities controlling your money or your financial decisions.

For the poor, life focuses on the ongoing cycle of income versus expenses where "breaking even" each month is the best scenario. These are the people who live paycheck to paycheck, often wryly complaining that they have "too much month left at the end of the money." In equation form, the financial position of the poor looks like this:

Income minus Expenses will equal $0 (or less).

Income for the poor comes primarily from a job. (At this time we are not considering other income sources such as public assistance or welfare because even these sources rarely change the overall equation.) A job can be defined essentially as, Just Over Broke. A fundamental maxim of financial success is that no one gets rich working for somebody else. Financially speaking, a job is a short-term fix to a long-term problem. The main reason people have jobs is because that is what they were taught. You grow up, go to school, graduate, get a job, work for 45 years (or longer), retire on a pension (maybe), die.

One of the secrets to financial success is learning to think, plan, and act beyond merely the present time and the week-to-week paycheck. This means, among other things, changing your habits of thought and action with regard to money. Your habits toward money either will keep you where you are or enable you to advance to progressively higher levels. Here is an example. Many poor people stay poor because they are in the habit of buying "stuff." What is "stuff"? "Stuff" is inexpensive things that people buy that they do not need for survival—but that eat up their limited resources anyway. Perhaps because they cannot afford anything else, or because they believe they are being frugal, they buy "stuff" at sales, discount houses, eBay, and other places, and always look for sale items wherever they shop. Looking for the best price is always a good idea, but the danger with sales and discounts is giving in to the temptation to buy "on sale" something you would not buy otherwise because you don't really need it. Where's the savings in buying something you don't need just because you got a "great price"?

Thinking of money only as something to use for paying bills and buying "stuff" is a mind-set that will keep you poor.

> **Thinking of money only as something to use for paying bills and buying "stuff" is a mind-set that will keep you poor.**

The Middle Class

The middle class is a significant step up from the poor, although there are still some similarities in thought and assumptions. One clear difference, at least on the surface, is that middle-class people have a healthier income/expense ratio. I say "on the surface" because appearances can be deceiving. In the eyes of the poor, and often in their own eyes as well, middle-class people frequently appear wealthier than they really are.

Like the poor, the emphasis in the mind of the middle class is on direct income generated by a job. The major difference is that middle-class income exceeds expenses, leaving some "free" money for flexibility that the poor do not have (at least theoretically). Expressed as an equation:

Income minus Expenses equals more than $0.

This "free" money left over after expenses gives middle-class people the flexibility to purchase assets to increase their prosperity, or so it appears. In reality, the true picture often is quite different. As I said before, the middle class often are mistaken for the wealthy. Why? Because of the "toys" they possess—the cars they drive; the clothes they wear; the houses they live in. Unfortunately, most of these "trappings" of success that they display have been purchased with borrowed money.

> *The poor have no assets, only expenses. The rich buy assets that make them richer. The middle class buy liabilities that they think are assets.*

The poor have no assets, only expenses. The rich buy assets that make them richer. The middle class buy liabilities that they think are assets. And therein lies the problem.

Remember, an asset is anything that pays you money, while a liability is anything that costs you money. A side-by-side comparison will help explain:

Assets	vs.	Liabilities
Put money in your pocket		Take money out of your pocket
Will feed you even if you stop working		Will eat you if you stop working
Examples		**Examples**
Savings account, IRA, business, rental property, etc.		Vacation home, boat RV, motorcycle, etc.

Everybody has liabilities. The secret to financial success is to minimize liabilities while maximizing assets. Many middle-class people understand this concept but never succeed in making it work because of their confusion between assets and liabilities. The best-case scenario is having enough true assets to cover all your liabilities.

But isn't a regular paycheck an asset? Not really. Consider this: What would happen if you could no longer work because of a severe injury or serious illness? How would you support yourself if you suddenly lost your paycheck? These are critical questions for the self-employed especially, who often face the very real danger of financial ruin if they can no longer work. Even if you go on permanent disability and receive social or supplemental security benefits, they will put you on a fixed income and severely restrict your financial flexibility unless you have income from another source that does not depend on your ability to work. In other words—assets. A regular paycheck is important as day-to-day and week-to-week "bread and butter" money, but don't make the mistake of thinking of it as an asset. Pay received from

> *Everybody has liabilities. The secret to financial success is to minimize liabilities while maximizing assets.*

an employer is not the vehicle for building true wealth or financial security.

The Rich

In contrast to the poor and the middle class, the rich and those in the process of becoming rich do not depend on a job for their financial security. They may have a job, but their financial security comes from other sources of income. The poor and the middle class work for money. When considering a job, they want to know how much it pays. The rich, however, do not work for money; they make money work for them by acquiring assets that will produce income automatically, thus building wealth. Another term for these wealth-creating assets is passive income.

> *The rich, however, do not work for money; they make money work for them by acquiring assets that will produce income automatically, thus building wealth.*

Passive income means that your money is working for you rather than you working for money. Financial freedom is gained when your passive income is greater than your expenses. Expressed as an equation, it looks like this:

Passive Income (Assets) is more than Expenses/Liabilities, which equals Freedom.

Edward Gibbon, author of the classic masterpiece, The Decline and Fall of the Roman Empire, described financial freedom this way:

I am indeed rich, since my income is superior to my expenses, and my expense is equal to my wishes.

Whether you are poor or middle class, the goal to becoming rich is to develop the habit of using your discretionary income (money left over after meeting needs and paying expenses) to acquire true assets (not liabilities masquerading as assets), which in turn will return to you more discretionary income, which is then used to invest in more assets, and so on. This is one of the essential differences between the rich and the non-rich, and it involves both mind-set

> *The goal to becoming rich is to develop the habit of using your discretionary income to acquire true assets, which in turn will return to you more discretionary income, which is then used to invest in more assets.*

and behavior. The non-rich spend their money on things that depreciate in value and return nothing, while the rich invest their money in assets that appreciate in value and return greater value than the amount invested. (I highly recommend that you read financial books by Robert Kiyosaki, including Rich Dad, Poor Dad, upon which much of this chapter's content is based.)

> *The non-rich spend their money on things that depreciate in value and return nothing, while the rich invest their money in assets that appreciate in value and return greater value than the amount invested.*

Everyone has to start somewhere. Like any other journey, the road to wealth begins with small steps. No matter where you are financially, you can take steps now to improve your situation and move you in the direction of your dreams. Developing a good budget will help you control spending and identify whatever discretionary income you have. Determine within yourself to invest that discretionary income, or a specific portion of it, in assets that will bring you positive returns and add money to your pocket. At first it may be as simple as a savings account to which you add money regularly and which earns interest (passive income). Don't worry if you have to start slowly or with a small amount of money. The important thing is to start now. Once you have started, be consistent. Save or invest regularly, no matter how little it may be. In the early stages, developing the habit is more important than the amount.

Financial freedom, which the truly rich enjoy, eliminates the need for a day-to-day job. When passive income exceeds expenses and liabilities, income from a job becomes icing on the cake. You can work because you want to, not because you have to. And you can focus on work that you love.

In fact, many of the truly wealthy, instead of working at a job, actually create jobs by owning and/or investing in corporation/business entities. By building wealth through sound financial planning and decisions, they move from being employees to being employers.

SAVING AND INVESTING FOR THE FUTURE

CHAPTER EIGHT

We all need to prepare for the future. Nature itself teaches us this lesson. Consider the lowly ant. Just as the ant instinctively and diligently saves up for the winter, we need to understand the importance of planning ahead and learn the principle of saving and investing. Such wise use of resources will bring about positive results for the future, while their unwise use will lead to negative consequences.

We can illustrate this lesson with a story. A rich man was about to go away on a business trip. Prior to his departure, he entrusted portions of his wealth to three of his servants. Allotting to each servant according to his ability, he gave $5,000 to the first servant, $2,000 to the second, and $1,000 to the third. After their master left on his trip, the first servant went out immediately and, through careful investing and trading, doubled his money. The second servant did the same. The third servant, however, fearing his master and afraid of what might happen if he lost the money he had been given, did nothing with it. He simply wrapped it up and buried it in the ground for safekeeping.

After a long while, the rich man returned home and called his three servants to account for their use of his money. The first servant proudly presented the $10,000 he had made, doubling his master's investment. Likewise, the second servant brought the $4,000 he had made. The master praised these two servants for their wise and able management and promoted them to greater responsibilities and privileges. The third servant, however, merely brought back the original $1,000 he had been given, making excuses about his master's hardness and his own fear of using the money. This brought an angry response from his master who said, "Even if you were afraid of me and afraid to invest the money, the least you could have done was deposit it in the bank so that it would have accrued some interest. The angry master then severely punished his lazy servant, demoting him, and taking from him the $1,000 he had been given; and then gave the $1,000 to the first servant, who already had $10,000. The moral of the story is that those who prove faithful with a little will be entrusted with more. In other words, the more money you make through wise investments and saving, the

> *Those who prove faithful with a little will be entrusted with more.*

more money you will have to invest. This story helps us understand the necessity of preparation, diligence, and planning where finances are concerned.

> *What we do with what we have now determines how much we will have in the future and how effective we will be in leaving a healthy legacy to future generations.*

In this story, each servant was given something—not equally, but each according to his ability. Likewise, every one of us has talents and gifts according to our ability, along with the potential to develop them more fully. There is no point or profit in fretting over what we have or do not have. It does not matter whether someone else has more or less than we do. What matters is that we learn how to use wisely what we have. What we do with what we have now determines how much we will have in the future and how effective we will be in leaving a healthy legacy to future generations.

An "Opportunity Cost"

Every money decision has a cost of its own, what we call an "opportunity cost." Simply stated, an "opportunity cost" refers to what we give up in order to get something else. In every choice, there is an opportunity cost. If you decide to go to college, for example, you are giving up the income you could have earned by working full-time during those years, plus whatever you could have purchased with the money used to attend school. You also may take on loans to pay for school, which will have to be paid back with future income that could have gone for other purposes.

The good news, of course, is that even with opportunity costs, college is usually a good idea for most people. The average graduate makes 70 percent more over his or her lifetime than someone who earns only a high school diploma. If, however, you train for a career that has little demand and wind up making the same amount as a high school grad or pile up huge amounts of student loan debt you can never repay, you may regret the money spent on school and the foregone income.

Understanding that our choices have opportunity costs, and examining what those costs are, should help us make better economic decisions.

Recommendations for a Savings Plan

A good man looks ahead to the future and makes a plan. He manages his money and his life in such a way that they impact future generations. Whereas, a selfish person lives only for today, expecting others to take care of him when he is old. In other words, a good man leaves an inheritance to his children's children.

Here are some helpful tips for developing a solid habit of saving your money and other financial resources:

1. Start saving now to build an emergency fund equal to at least four to eight months of living expenses.

2. As a rule, a minimum of ten percent of your income should always go towards saving regularly.

3. Most people follow the "deferment plan" when it comes to saving—in other words, they will do it when things get better. Then one day they wake up much older and nothing has been set aside. No matter what your circumstances or the level of your resources, there is no better time to start saving than today—right now. Start saving something, no matter how little. Even a few dollars a week is better than nothing at all. At the very least it helps develop the habit of saving.

> *Now is the time; today is the day to start saving something, no matter how little.*

4. Be sure to save weekly, and don't miss. People accumulate wealth little by little; it doesn't just happen.

Dangerous Attitudes Regarding Money

Kept in perspective and used properly, money can be very beneficial and help many people. Used incorrectly, however, it can lead to destruction. With this in mind, here are a few dangers to watch out for regarding money.

1. Worshipping money—making money your god. The riches of the world give false security. Our riches will fail us whenever we need them the most. The wisest approach is always to remember that money is not an end in itself but a tool to be used to build for

> *Money is not an end in itself but a tool to be used to build for the future and for the benefit of others.*

the future and for the benefit of others.

2. Regarding poverty as spiritual… or as sinful. Some people think that money is evil. However, money is intrinsically neither moral nor immoral. Morality applies only in the attitude we have concerning it. For example, some people equate a lack of material things—in other words, poverty—with spirituality. They think that in order to be spiritual, they have to be poor. On the other hand, some people believe that a lack of material things indicates wrongdoing in a person's life. Poverty is not essentially wrong; however, there is a time in a person's life when it is wrong to struggle financially. Poverty has many shortcomings. It hinders blessings in our lives and the ability to be useful in many different ways.

We need to recognize the many beneficial things that money can do, such as build hospitals, schools, and training centers. It takes finances to do good work. Money becomes evil only when we allow it to control us. Again, money is a tool to use in this life only, because it will not follow us into the next life. We come into the world with nothing and we take nothing when we die. As newborn babies, we enter this world with gripping hands, but we will leave it with our hands extended. We come in trying to get everything we can and trying to get ahead, but we always have to give everything up and leave it behind when we depart this life.

3. Desiring more and more. Remember, money is only a means to an end. Possessions never make a person happy or content. Besides, the more possessions we have, the more time it takes to take care of them. If we are not careful, they will end up owning us, and we will be their slaves. Those who consider spending and buying as fun or as a way to help them feel better are deceived. There is no lasting pleasure or health in things.

Wise philosophers throughout the ages have said that human life does not consist in the abundance of the things we possess. The more we have, the more we want; and the more we obtain, the more we have to lose. Those who want more just work and work to obtain objects they never get to enjoy.

> *The more possessions we have, the more time it takes to take care of them. If we are not careful, they will end up owning us, and we will be their slave.*

4. Hoarding and being greedy. Greed is an insatiable hunger that is never satisfied, no matter how often or how much it is fed. That is why greedy people are never happy; their constant hunger for more consumes them from within even as they continue to feed it from without. And what good is it to keep to ourselves more abundance than we will ever be able to use? Would it not be better to be liberal with our abundance so that others can be blessed by our generosity?

5. Dishonesty. If you have a lack of money, you must not lie, cheat, steal, or be dishonest in any way in order to get more or to avoid paying. Pay all your debts no matter how long it takes or how difficult it may be. Dishonesty has a way of catching up with you eventually, and its cost is always calculated in more than dollars and cents, such as reputation, integrity, respect, and peace of mind. It is only right to be just toward all men and give them what you owe. Do not withhold good from those to whom it is due, especially when you are in the position to do something about it. Give it promptly.

6. Self-sufficiency. If you have an abundance, avoid thinking that you have enough money to take care of your own situations. Beware! History clearly shows that reversals of fortune and finances can and do come suddenly and unexpectedly, wiping out everything that we expected to last a lifetime. This is another reason for investing, saving, and advanced planning—to secure your resources in financial instruments and assets that are shielded from the effects of economic downturns.

Steps to Financial Freedom

In addition to watching out for the dangers associated with money, it is just as important to make positive plans for achieving financial freedom. Here are some tips.

1. Plan your financial independence. Financial planning is a process; it takes careful thought followed by deliberate action. Many people desire financial freedom but never seem to get around to doing anything about it. There is no better time to plan for the future than now. There is never a better time to invest than the present. If you try to hit the lows in real estate or in the stock market, you are going to miss. Start now and don't wait for a better time. There is none.

> *There is no better time to plan for the future than now.*

2. If you want your plan to succeed, it will take commitment, discipline, and sacrifice. It will involve the whole family. It will require a written plan, something visual that will show you how you are progressing.

3. Successful planning involves educating yourself about investments. It's important to know how different investments work. There is safety in diversification, so you will need to establish a balanced portfolio. In order to do so, you need to know how your investing relates to your tax situation and how tax laws work. Understand inflation, the rise and fall of stock markets, and your investing objectives. Don't be dismayed if all this sounds complicated. Learning about these topics may not be something on which you can or want to spend your time. In that case, call on the expertise of a trustworthy financial counselor or tax consultant to guide you. Be sure in any case, however, that ultimately you take personal responsibility for making your own decisions as to where and how much to invest.

4. Goals must be realistic and attainable. Develop a plan that will work. If your plan is unattainable, you will get frustrated and quit. Be sure it's measurable and within reach. Begin by establishing and pursuing short-term goals such as:

- **Charitable contributions.**
- **Keeping current bills paid on time.**
- **Taxes to be paid.**
- **Savings and retirement.**

Next, add long-term goals such as:

- **Children's college education.**
- **Investments: stocks or real estate.**
- **Owning your own home.**
- **Starting your own business.**
- **Participating in charitable projects.**

The Pyramid of Peace

CHAPTER NINE

Many people, instead of planning deliberately and carefully for the future, depend on and place their hopes of prosperity on unlikely dreams such as winning a large amount of money through gambling, or receiving a large inheritance. Speaking of inheritance, it is foolish for an elderly person to leave an inheritance to his or her grown children, who are often elderly themselves. The best time to leave an inheritance to our children is while they are still young and growing, so we can enjoy watching them use it.

Wise and solid financial planning can help make this a reality. It also goes a long way in helping to establish peace in our lives; and if we are at peace with life, life goes a whole lot better.

> *The best time to leave an inheritance to our children is while they are still young and growing, so we can enjoy watching them use it.*

Building a Solid Foundation

How do we build stability in our financial lives? We start by laying down a solid foundation.

No structure, regardless of size or extravagance, will stand long if it is not erected on a good foundation. Architecturally speaking, a pyramid is the soundest structure that can be built. Has a pyramid ever been destroyed in a storm? I don't think so. The great pyramids of Egypt have stood for 4,000 years. A pyramid is not affected or blown over by the wind. Its foundation is secure. So, when we talk about building financial security in life, it is helpful to use the illustration of a pyramid.

At one time, I owned a four million-dollar company. During a trip to Kenya, I developed a business plan that I believed would increase my company to twenty million dollars within five years. When I brought the plan home, I hired professionals to review it. They told me that the business had a great foundation, but there was one problem—it was being built straight up. A better approach, they said, was to broaden the base so that I could rebuild and be much more likely to attain my goal.

This was hard for me because it meant I had to be willing to relinquish some authority, dispense power to some of my employees, and allow them to share the responsibility. In essence, I was to simply "steer the ship." These professionals also impressed upon me that, although I had built a great company, setbacks would still occur. Various elements would come against the business that could destroy it if it was not prepared to weather the storm. Regardless of how strong it was at the bottom, the taller it was, the more likely it would be to topple. By broadening the base, however, I could strengthen the entire structure so that if a certain area was hit, the whole company would not collapse.

There were times when I ran into extreme difficulty in a certain area, but the company still grew in the midst of that problem. The strength of the entire business overcame the effects of the problem, and the company continued to grow in spite of it.

Plan to Succeed

Some people succeed because they are destined to, but most people succeed because they are determined to. Unless you have a great inheritance coming your way, it will be necessary for you to plan to be successful. Only five percent of people actually achieve financial independence in life. Financial independence is when your investment net worth is generating the annual income on which you need to live. This is not a job. If you reach this stage, you are beyond a job; you are free to choose what to do with your time.

> *Some people succeed because they are destined to, but most people succeed because they are determined to.*

Financial success is a lot like building a house. Just as you cannot build a house without a plan, you cannot achieve financial success unless you know clearly where you are going and how to get there. You need a blueprint, and you always begin with the foundation.

Most people accept what life gives them and don't bother to plan. Money is a real teacher. You must learn how to make money. The way you make and spend money reflects who you are: your values, your morals, and your integrity. The way you save money, the way you share it with others, the way you open your hand to it or block its flow—all these reveal your character. If you scoop up sand in your hand, the more you try to hold it, the more it slips away. With an open hand, however, you can pile up more and more sand. In the same way, most people try to squeeze their finances to make them stretch,

> *The way to make your finances grow is by being liberal with what you have, using wisdom and discretion, giving with a cheerful heart.*

83

when in reality the way to make your finances grow is by being liberal with what you have, not foolishly casting it away in every direction or for every scheme or need that comes along, but with wisdom and discretion, giving with a cheerful heart.

Financial Peace Pyramid

The key to financial success is to build what I will call a Financial Peace Pyramid. Webster's Dictionary defines the verb pyramid as meaning, "to increase rapidly and progressively step by step on a broad base." Pyramids always have wide, secure foundations. The foundation of your Financial Peace Pyramid consists of four essential "stones": home, reserve, insurance, and will.

Home

A home of your own—one that you have purchased—will help bring security to your life. Most people don't think about the home they live in as an investment or a building block for personal financial prosperity and peace. The truth is, however, that the home you live in is the first building block of the pyramid of your financial stability. Your home is the most basic need you have for shelter and also financial independence. And if you are like most people, your home mortgage will be the largest financial obligation you incur. Your mortgage payment will cost you more in interest than any other purchase you make.

Although your personal home will comprise the largest single commitment of your resources, it is also the one that will give the biggest return on your investment. Owning a home is like forced savings. It is a great investment and an excellent tax shelter. Real estate grows faster and more steadily than any other asset. In addition, as you regularly make payments on your mortgage each month, you gradually and steadily build equity in your home.

Owning your own home is a great source of personal peace and satisfaction, but you will have even more peace if it is debt-free. One worthy goal to set in personal financial security is to pay off your home mortgage ahead of schedule. This will give you the assurance of having a roof over your head while at the same time reducing your monthly living expenses.

All in all, a home is the greatest investment most people will ever make. Your home, therefore, is the first building block upon which you build your financial security.

Reserve

Work hard to build up a reserve in savings equal to four to eight months of living expenses. In today's economy, jobs are not secure. If you are not prepared and a problem arises, your foundation will crumble. Hence, this reserve is so crucial for financial peace.

Most people have the tendency to spend money when they have it, and starve and complain when they run out. If you are wise, you will take some portion of every paycheck and invest it in some way so that you can build wealth. Living from paycheck to paycheck makes financial peace in your life impossible because you will always be stressed out over finances and trying to make ends meet. Also, you might come across the deal of a lifetime, but without a reserve, you will have to charge the payments to your credit card. If you have to use a credit card in order to buy an item, you can't afford it. The reason so many people get into financial trouble is because they lie to themselves about their financial status. They think they will make the credit card payment when it comes due, but end up paying only the minimum. Their foundation starts on a lie and builds on a lie. There is no integrity in this.

We need to return to a cash society where we feel the pain every time we pay for something. So often we lie to impress others. When you go out to eat and pay for a meal with a credit card, you are lying to your friends. Simply paying cash for everything will go a long way toward bringing financial order to your life. The Financial Peace Pyramid must be built on truth and integrity. There is no integrity when you're out spending money you don't have. You are taking your future and bringing it into today, believing the lie that the future will be better than today. You are borrowing against your future because you believe you will get a raise and everything will increase.

Whereas, when you pile up a cash reserve through savings and discipline, you are less likely to throw money away on impulsive consumer spending. Saving is done with a vision toward financial independence and will encourage you to be more responsible.

> *We need to return to a cash society where we feel the pain every time we pay for something.*

Insurance

Insurance of any kind is a type of rented reserve fund. Most of us cannot afford to withstand the cost of replacing damages to our vehicles or homes or setbacks to our health, so it is wise to rent that reserve in the form of insurance policies. Insurance takes the relatively small risk of individuals and spreads it over thousands or even millions of people. We can therefore purchase a large amount of peace for a small amount of money.

In America, you can insure yourself against anything and everything, from health care to floods. Insurance is a way to cover the sudden and catastrophic losses through accidents and misfortune. Insurance will bring a lot of peace to your life because you know that your most important and valuable assets—your house and your health, for example—are protected.

If you own a business, you owe it to yourself and everyone who works for you to make sure that if you make a mistake or a serious reversal comes, everyone is fully covered. A business owner with integrity will make sure that everyone is well covered, particularly anyone who is injured or disabled due to a work-related accident. This not only helps protect you in the event of a lawsuit, but it is also the right thing to do. Someone who loses or suffers diminished earning capacity due to an accident while working for you deserves to be taken care of. Insurance also protects you against the unknown. Once you begin to develop wealth, you have different reasons for safeguarding yourself with a substantial amount of insurance.

Will

A will is a legal document allowing you to determine how your wealth will be distributed after your death. In many countries, if you do not have a will, your government will make those decisions for you. No matter what you have built, it will not be properly passed on. Consequently, you will have nothing to give to the next generation. Approximately 75 percent of people do not have a will at the time of their death. Subsequently, governments end up with millions of dollars every year. Most people don't like to deal with this subject because it reminds them of their own mortality. Death is inevitable, however, so it makes sense to prepare for it. Lack of a will can lead to a lot of fighting and misunderstanding between family and heirs left behind. It is good to remember that a will can be changed, updated, or restructured as needed, depending on changing circumstances.

> *Most people don't like to deal with the subject of a will because it reminds them of their own mortality. Death is inevitable, however, so it makes sense to prepare for it.*

If you try building your pyramid without these four foundational stones, the higher you build, the more likely your pyramid will topple, just like a house with no foundation will be blown over in a storm. Build right or your financial house will crumble.

Building Your Financial Pyramid

Everyone wants financial peace, but few are truly willing to pay the price to get it. Commitment is required. Laying a solid foundation of home, reserve, insurance, and will is the first step in that commitment. Once the foundation is laid, we can begin building the pyramid upward. The Financial Peace Pyramid has three levels that rise successively from the foundation upward: Conservative, Enterprising, and Speculative.

Conservative

This is the first level of the pyramid, built directly on top of the foundation. It is the lowest, most basic level of investing and carries the lowest risk, which is why it is called "Conservative." On this level, you focus on such financial matters as establishing a savings account, money market accounts, and buying bonds, mutual funds, utility company stock, CDs, treasury bonds, and fixed annuities. Conservative investing carries very low risk, but consequently does not provide a lot of reward. It is steady, however, and therefore a very good place to start. And certainly it is a far cry better than doing nothing. A solid lower level of conservative investments provides a strong base to support the riskier but more rewarding investments higher up.

There are multitudes of ways that you can divide an investment amount. The following is a guideline, just one example of a breakdown of a conservative investment:

- **20% money market.**
- **20% high quality bonds.**
- **25% growth and income funds.**
- **15% utilities.**
- **10% CDs.**
- **10% growth funds.**

The greatest benefit for the investor at any level is diversification.

Enterprising

The second level of the pyramid is "Enterprising." At this level you buy stocks, pay dividends, buy blue chip stocks, rental properties (real estate), gold and silver stocks, growth mutual funds, and perhaps start your own business. Again, here is a suggested breakdown for diversification:

- **30% blue chip stocks.**
- **25% growth and income funds.**
- **15% international funds/rental properties.**
- **15% precious metal funds.**
- **15% small cap funds.**

Investments at this level are somewhat riskier than at the Conservative level, but they bring higher returns.

Speculative

At this highest level of the Financial Peace Pyramid, you invest in high-risk ventures that also carry lucrative returns. Investments at this level include gas or oil wells, raw land, commercial real estate, penny stocks, tech stocks, building and selling in construction, and owning gold and silver coins.

There will be a number of disadvantages to every investment opportunity at every level, so make your investment decisions according to how much risk you are willing to bear. The greater the risk, the greater the rewards. Those investments at the top of the pyramid pay the most. The safer your investment, the less return you will receive. Conservative investments include a low risk with the lowest rewards, but don't spurn them for that reason. You need to build securely at the lower level so you can move confidently to the higher levels. I asked a gentleman one time how much I should invest in the stock market. His response was, "Whatever you are willing to lose." Conservative level investments are very safe. At the Enterprising and Speculative levels, however, invest only what you can afford to lose. Otherwise you will always be worrying about your investments. Ask yourself what you are willing to lose and build accordingly. Some people are comfortable investing heavily in high-risk instruments; others are not. Invest according to your stress level.

TURNING RICHES INTO WEALTH

CHAPTER TEN

Contrary to what many people assume, being rich and being wealthy are not necessarily the same. By "rich" I am referring to financial affluence, possession of large amounts of money and physical assets. "Wealth," on the other hand, refers to something deeper, something less tangible than money. Wealth goes beyond money and the mere possession of it. By this distinction, some who are rich are not wealthy, and some who are wealthy are not rich. Riches relate to balance sheets and the bottom line; wealth relates to profit sharing. Riches have to do with what you take in; wealth, with what you give back. The essential difference between riches and wealth hinges on two factors: income distribution and liberality.

Rich people can hoard their riches, and focus on increasing their own affluence and security and that of their immediate family with no care for anyone else. In doing so, they reveal that, while they are rich in the goods and possessions of the world, they are poverty-stricken in their souls.

Wealthy people, on the other

> **Riches have to do with what you take in; wealth, with what you give back.**

91

hand, regard their affluence as an opportunity and a privilege to bless others. They understand that riches are not for the purpose of being hoarded, but shared so that they can bless others as they themselves have been blessed. It all comes down to the attitude and condition of the

> *Generous people give because they are generous, not because of what they have or do not have.*

heart. Rich people can be stingy due to a selfish heart, while the wealthy proceed from a heart of liberality and generosity. This attitude is not reserved for those with a lot of money. A generous heart is independent of financial status. Generous people give because they are generous, not because of what they have or do not have. This is why those who hold off on giving until they "get

> *He who is not liberal with what he has only deceives himself by thinking he would be more liberal if he had more.*

more money" are only fooling themselves. Indeed, he who is not liberal with what he has only deceives himself by thinking he would be more liberal if he had more.

Liberality, of course, has to do with giving, which brings us full circle back to what we discussed in Chapter Two of this book.

Generous and liberal giving yields greater generosity and liberality. It's all about the scoop! In other words, the bigger the scoop you use to pour out from your substance onto others freely and willingly, the bigger the scoop that will return blessing to you—except in even greater measure. As illogical as this sounds, it is an ancient and time-tested principle. We receive according to what and how we give. The size and quality of the harvest we reap depends on the nature of our seeds and the liberality with which we sow them.

Basic Income Distribution

Ideally, every household budget should contain three basic elements: fixed expenses, variable expenses, and savings. Most people, however, have little or no savings in their everyday budget and no systematic plan for building savings into the future. All of their money is tied up in fixed and variable expenses. This is an unhealthy financial state that must be corrected as a fundamental second step toward financial success.

In the breakdown that follows, all percentages will vary according to your income level and according to where you live. In addition, all percentages are based on gross income (from all sources before taxes are deducted), not net income.

Charitable Contributions: Ten Percent (10%)

Many people who say that they will give to charitable causes never follow through, because they do not have a specific plan in place to do so. Although our charitable giving should always be from the heart and given freely, the best way to ensure that we do so is to regard charitable contributions as a fixed expense in our budget so we will be more likely to give regularly and consistently. Another advantage to budgeting our charitable contributions is that it helps us determine a realistic level of giving—a level that is in line with our income as well as our other financial obligations. Ten percent is a good basic level, but don't consider it etched in stone. As circumstances demand, you may give more or less. It is important to have a definite plan in place for giving. A good rule of thumb for determining your level of giving is to ask yourself, "Without endangering my own or my family's financial situation, how much can I give and still remain willing and cheerful in the giving?"

Savings: Ten Percent (10%)

Setting aside savings in a deliberate, consistent, and systematic manner is just as important as having a deliberate plan for charitable giving. Both ancient and modern teachings reveal the wisdom of setting aside assets during times of plenty in anticipation of seasons of want. Save now while times are good so that you will have assets on hand when times aren't so good.

The savings I am talking about here consist primarily of "liquid cash"—readily available money in a savings account or money market account set aside for emergencies or other unanticipated expenses. As a minimum, four to eight months' worth of living expenses should be maintained at all times. It is at this one point where most family financial crises occur. Many families can get by okay without savings—as long as everything runs smoothly. But sooner or later a problem will come up, an emergency financial need, such as a major car repair or medical expense, and they have no money to pay for it. So, they either pull money from a fixed expense and fall behind in other payments, or they go into debt. Either way, they're in trouble.

If you do not currently have four to eight months of living expenses in reserve, start now to build toward that goal. Depending on your circumstances, it may take a while to get there, but there is no better time than now to begin.

Taxes: Thirty Percent (30%)

Regardless of how we may feel about paying taxes, it is the law as well as a vital part of responsible citizenship. This thirty percent (30%) block, set aside for taxes includes taxes of every kind:

- **Income (federal, state, local).**
- **Capital gains.**
- **Sales.**

- **Property.**
- **School.**
- **Vehicle.**

Normally, income taxes are withheld automatically from your paycheck unless you are self-employed, but they should still be considered in your overall income/expense picture.

Committed Debt: Thirty-five Percent (35%)

We have a moral and ethical obligation to pay everyone what we owe. To do otherwise makes us no better than a thief.

Committed debt includes such things as:

- **Home (mortgage or rent).**
- **Household expenses (repairs and upkeep).**
- **Car payment.**
- **Consumer debt (credit cards, bank loans, etc.).**

As we have already noted, consumer debt ideally should not be in the picture, but because it is a reality in almost every family, I have included it here. If consumer debt is part of your "committed debt," you should put a plan into place to eliminate that debt as quickly and systematically as possible. If you have no consumer debt, you are already one giant step ahead, with more money available either to apply to other committed debt or to invest.

> *We have a moral and ethical obligation to pay everyone what we owe. To do otherwise makes us no better than a thief.*

Variable Expenses: Fifteen Percent (15%)

Distributing income according to the preceding allotments

leaves fifteen percent (15%) of gross income for "variable" expenses: one-time or infrequent expenditures or regular expenditures with costs that vary from month to month. Variable expenses include such items as:

- **Food.**
- **Clothing.**
- **Gifts.**
- **Insurance.**
- **Seed.**

Notice that "seed money" for investment purposes comes from this portion of income. Because all other categories are fixed, it is from here that discretionary funds must come. It stands to reason that the more the committed debt category can be reduced, the more discretionary funds will become available and, consequently, the more seed money that will be on hand.

The Life of the Seed

Never underestimate the importance or power of the seed. It contains life for you, your children, your grandchildren, and many others whom you can influence with your life and resources. The seed we sow willingly and joyfully will bless others and return multiplied blessings to us. It is through this avenue of liberality that wealth is built. Seed can be sown (invested) in many ways:

> *The seed we sow willingly and joyfully will bless others and return multiplied blessings to us.*

- **Businesses.**
- **Property.**

- **Stocks and Bonds.**
- **Charities.**
- **Other.**

Likewise, the harvest of seed returned can take many different forms:

- **Cash gifts.**
- **Bonuses.**
- **Dividends.**
- **Profits.**
- **Interest.**
- **Refunds.**

All of these and more comprise a harvest that blesses many and provides new seed for further sowing, thus producing a continuous cycle where liberal sowing leads to abundant harvesting.

Minimizing Misfortune

Setbacks and difficulties are inevitable in the financial realm as in every other area of life. The wise financial planner anticipates misfortune and makes preparations in advance to minimize it. This isn't pessimism; it's realism. So how do we prepare for misfortune? Here are four steps.

> *The wise financial planner anticipates misfortune and makes preparations in advance to minimize it. This isn't pessimism; it's realism.*

1. Maintain a balanced portfolio.

Distributing your money across several areas reduces the risk of substantial loss. As the old adage says, "Don't put all your eggs in the same basket." There is strength in numbers and in diversity. This will help ensure secure investments as well as strong relationships.

2. Practice strategic planning.

What worked yesterday may not work tomorrow. Don't get locked into small-minded or short-sighted thinking. Study the markets and other financial indicators. Learn to anticipate trends and future trouble spots and plan accordingly. A trained and trusted financial advisor can help with this.

3. Invest long-term.

Sow with the harvest in mind rather than second-guessing your investment. You cannot predict the cycle of each investment, so choose them wisely and stick with them. Invest only according to your personal level of comfort and then resist the temptation to sell off your investments just because things appear to be taking a downward turn. History shows that the most successful investors are those who choose carefully and then persevere through good times and bad.

4. Seize opportunities.

There are opportunities all around. The key is to become aware of them and be prepared for them so that you can seize them when they present themselves. It will take courage and confidence. The next chapter is dedicated to the power of an opportunity.

The Power of an Opportunity

Chapter Eleven

What separates the successful from the unsuccessful? Why do some people succeed while others do not? There could be many reasons: motivation, passion, education. One of the most significant factors is that successful people know how to recognize and seize opportunities when they appear, while unsuccessful people do not. Opportunities abound for those who know how to look for them. Although the timing of opportunities cannot be predicted, it is possible to prepare ahead of time for when they do come.

> **Although the timing of opportunities cannot be predicted, it is possible to prepare ahead of time for when they do come.**

There is power in an opportunity. Depending on the circumstances, an opportunity met or missed can be life-changing. One key to seizing opportunities is to realize that they often appear in unexpected ways or in an unexpected form. Failure to recognize this fact can lead to a missed opportunity.

In 1995, I had been invited to travel to South Africa for the first time in my life. I gave little or almost no thought to this invitation and made a hasty decision to decline the offer. I had no desire to travel that far during that time of my life; nor did I want to go to a country I had no interest in; nor did I see any advantage in spending time in a place where I knew absolutely no one.

Six months later, I was presented with the same invitation. This time, I hesitated before making a decision. When the same proposal was extended to me a second time, I paid more attention. It didn't take long before I decided I had better accept the offer. The end result was that, because I was willing to travel to an unfamiliar place, I was able to eventually purchase four game farms, several apartment complexes, and houses—all in South Africa.

> *Opportunities often appear in unexpected ways or in an unexpected form.*

Here is my point. Opportunities often appear in unexpected ways or in an unexpected form. We miss some good fortune because the opportunity comes in a much different way than we had expected it to. It may involve people we don't care for or situations that we are unfamiliar or uncomfortable with. Hence, we immediately disregard the potential of the experience. I almost missed my chance because I saw and concentrated on a risk that I wasn't willing to take. In my mind, South Africa was an unknown location occupied by unknown people. Fortunately, I put aside my lack of knowledge, shifted my perspective, traveled to a far-away country, and realized a substantial profit through acquiring several real estate properties.

However, my narrow, fixed expectations almost cost me the chance of a lifetime. Once I saw things from a different perspective, I recognized the opportunity that was mine and seized it.

Narrow vision can be our greatest enemy in recognizing and seizing opportunities. We can be sidetracked by pride, prejudiced thinking, or other limitations and consequently miss wonderful opportunities for growth and increase that may come our way.

This is why we need wisdom in our finances and every other area of life. Wise people expect, prepare for, and look for opportunities...and then grab hold of them as they come by.

Webster's Dictionary defines opportunity as "a good chance for advancement or progress." In this life, time is all we have and opportunities are what we get to make our time on earth meaningful and significant. Life, then, is a collection of seasons of taken or missed opportunities. It is opportunities met or missed that determine our success or failure.

> **Life is a collection of seasons of taken or missed opportunities.**

Opportunities are time sensitive. The opportunity of a lifetime must be seized during the lifetime of that opportunity. It may never come again. If we do not seize the opportunity while it is there, we must live with the consequences of our inactivity, possibly for the rest of our lives. The big challenge of opportunities is that they will always take us out of our comfort zone. Some people don't want to be made uncomfortable, which is why they never succeed. Oprah Winfrey, a successful American business entrepreneur, has said, "Success comes when preparation and opportunity meet." It is a true statement.

> **The opportunity of a lifetime must be seized during the lifetime of that opportunity.**

Opportunities, then, are stepping-stones on the way to success. They are vehicles to help us get where we are going. Sometimes, opportunities may be small or appear not to hold much promise. Don't let that bother you. Remember, an egg may be small and fragile, but it is destined to fly.

> **An egg may be small and fragile, but it is destined to fly.**

101

Enemies of Opportunity

The flipside of learning to recognize opportunity—and just as important for success—is learning to anticipate and recognize enemies of opportunity and to make advance preparations for dealing with them. Here are a few.

1. Opposition

You will never be the person you can be if pressure, tension, and discipline are taken out of your life. We all need opposition and obstacles in our way to strengthen us and hone our skills. In order to get honey, you must have bees.

2. Procrastination

Oftentimes, we know what to do but we keep postponing until the opportunity is lost. While we are procrastinating, life speeds by. Remaining inactive or indecisive because something seems too difficult eventually makes it impossible. There is no time like the present. In fact, the present is all the time we have. The past is gone and the future is beyond our immediate reach. There is only now.

> *The present is all the time we have. The past is gone and the future is beyond our immediate reach. There is only now.*

3. Excuses

Someone said that an excuse is the skin of a reason stuffed with a lie. As long as you continue to make excuses about why you can't do something, you will never do it. Do any of these sound familiar?

- **"I don't have the money."**

  Start with what you do have—and build.

• **"I don't have any contacts."**

Join a professional organization in your field or area of interest. Subscribe to a professional journal. Attend a conference or workshop. Start building a network.

• **"I can't quit my job because I have to support my family."**

Start slow and take it as you go. Most successful businesses and other ventures began that way.

• **"I'm not smart enough."**

Consider taking continuing education classes. Challenge yourself with something new. Expand your horizons.

• **"I don't have the time; I'm too busy."**

Rearrange your priorities. Find nonessential time-consumers that you can eliminate. You will make time for whatever is truly important to you.

• **"I don't have enough money saved."**

You may not need much to get started. If you do, consider trying to find a partner or an investor to share the cost.

• **"It takes too long to build a business."**

Anything worth doing takes time.

• **"I'm afraid. It's too risky."**

Risk is a part of life. Nothing worthwhile comes without risk, especially success.

• "I don't like dealing with employees."

Don't put the cart before the horse. If you're just starting out, it may be a while before this situation even becomes an issue. Down the road, when you have built some success—and some confidence— you likely will feel differently about it.

• "I'm too old or too young."

You're never too young or too old to start making positive changes in your life.

• "I'll have to go back to school first."

If that idea seems daunting, consider starting with one class at a time. Give yourself time to adjust to the idea of being back in school, then pick up the pace.

4. Unbelief

You've got to believe in yourself. Otherwise, you will never accomplish anything worthwhile for yourself or for those you love. You will never rise above your internal belief system. Garrison Keillor, an American author, musician, and radio personality, once said, "Sometimes you have to look reality in the eye and deny it." No matter how imposing or impossible the challenges you face may appear, the moment you tell yourself, "I'm going to do this," answers to those challenges will start revealing themselves.

5. Fear

Fear is an acid that is pumped into one's atmosphere. It causes mental and moral suffocation and death to energy and all growth. Unchecked, fear will lead you into poverty! Many times, what separates success from failure is action. When you confront your fears with action, it will drive out your insecurity. Action breeds confidence, which comes by doing. Remember, most of your fears rarely come to pass.

Here are some common fears that you must overcome:

- **Fear of success.** Some people are afraid to succeed because their lives are centered around the struggle. Without the struggle, life loses meaning.

- **Fear of failure.** Failure is a temporary setback. Failure is never permanent unless you allow it to keep you from getting up again. In a way, failure is a success in that it teaches you what not to do. Failure can be a success if you learn from it.

- **Fear of rejection.** Don't become too concerned about what other people think. This is your vision, not theirs.

- **Fear of risk.** As I said before, risk is part of life. Nothing good comes without risk. When you try anything, there is always risk. But the saddest outcome in life is to risk nothing. When you risk nothing, you do nothing. Subsequently, you have nothing, and you are nothing.

- **Fear of the unknown.** You may not know the future, but your attitude and faith in yourself will determine whether you face the future with trepidation or with confidence.

6. Past Failures

Allowing your past failures to dictate your present decisions will paralyze your future. Stop blaming the past for your current status. Your past is no indication of your future.

7. Lack of Courage

Courage is the mental or moral strength to venture, persevere, and withstand danger, fear, or difficulty. Many people who rose to success overcame their weakness and fears. One distinctive characteristic of courage is the willingness to accept personal responsibility. Someone once said, "A man can fail many times, but he isn't a failure until he begins to blame someone else." Courage is absolutely essential if you hope to succeed in finances and in life.

CONCLUSION

Be a dreamer, for a dreamer sees the opportunity, and not the obstacle. Don't allow opposition to discourage you. Many times, conflict or restraint is simply an indicator that you are on the right track.

Opportunities are stepping-stones to your destination, yet you must first recognize them and seize them. Be alert, for opportunities are all around you. Nevertheless, they will not last forever, and they seldom knock twice.

Contact Author:

www.eugenestrite.com

Generation Culture Transformation
Specializing in publishing for generation culture change

Visit us Online at:
www.egenco.com
www.egenbooks.com

Write to: eGen Co. LLC
824 Tallow Hill Road
Chambersburg, PA 17202 USA
Phone: 717-461-3436
Email: info@egenco.com

 facebook.com/egenbooks

 twitter.com/vishaljets

youtube.com/egenpub

 egenco.com/blog